INCREDIBLE
MYSTERIES
OF THE
BIBLE

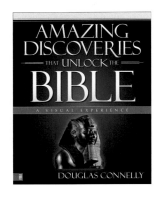

Amazing Discoveries That Unlock the Bible
Douglas Connelly
ISBN 978-0-310-25799-8

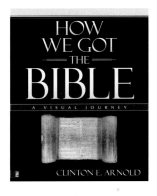

How We Got the Bible
Clinton E. Arnold
ISBN 978-0-310-25306-8

INCREDIBLE MYSTERIES

OF THE

BIBLE

A VISUAL EXPLORATION

STEPHEN M. MILLER

ZONDERVAN®

ZONDERVAN.com/
AUTHORTRACKER
follow your favorite authors

ZONDERVAN

Incredible Mysteries of the Bible
Copyright © 2008 by Stephen M. Miller

Requests for information should be addressed to:

Zondervan, *Grand Rapids, Michigan 49530*

Library of Congress Cataloging-in-Publication Data

Miller, Stephen M., 1952–
    Incredible mysteries of the Bible : a visual exploration / Stephen M. Miller.
       p. cm. — (Zondervan visual reference series)
       ISBN 978-0-310-25594-9
    1. Bible—Miscellanea 2. Bible—Criticism, interpretation, etc. I. Title.
  BS615.M54 2007
  220 — dc22

2007000428

Published in association with the literary agency of Alive Communications, Inc., 7680 Goddard Street, Suite 200, Colorado Springs, CO 80920, www.alivecommunications.com.

Interior design by Ron Huizenga

Printed in Hong Kong

09 10 11 12 13 14 15 16 17 18 19 20 21 22 • 36 35 34 33 32 31 30 29 28 27 26 25 24 24 23 22 21 20 19 18 17 16 15 14 13 12 11 10 9 8 7 6 5 4 3 2

TABLE OF CONTENTS

WHERE WAS THE GARDEN OF EDEN?

OCEAN OR MOUNTAINS There are two competing theories at the moment. The garden of Eden was either located in what is now the Persian Gulf, or in the mountains of northern Iran, near the Ararat range where Noah's ark came to a rest.

There's not much to go on in the Bible except the names of four rivers. All four sprang from an unnamed river that watered the garden and then flowed out, splitting four ways. Two of those rivers are well known: the Tigris and Euphrates that empty into the Persian Gulf. But two remain a mystery: the Pishon and Gihon.

UNDERWATER One theory says the Persian Gulf was once a fertile river valley, and home to Eden. Flooding—perhaps from a cataclysmic deluge or from melting polar ice that lifted the sea levels—inundated the valley and linked it with the Arabian Sea, creating the gulf and burying Eden.

The lost river of Pishon may have been what is now the dried up fossil of a river in Kuwait: Wadi al Batin. The lost Gihon may have been Iran's only navigable river: the Karun. Thousands of animal remains in the Gulf area suggest it was once home to a forest of plants and animals.

IN THE MOUNTAINS This theory places Eden on the high plains of a mountain range where the Tigris and Euphrates start—700 miles north of the Persian Gulf.

There, near the Iranian industrial town of Tabriz, flow two more rivers—some say the lost rivers of Eden. The Gihon may be the river called Giahun before the Islamic invasion of the seventh century AD; it's now called Aras. The Pishon may be the former Uizhun, with the "P" switched to "U" to accommodate the Iranian alphabet. The river is now called Uzun, with an added first name: Kezel, which means "golden." Genesis said the Pishon flowed around a land rich in gold—as does the Kezel Uzun, or the Golden Pishon if this theory is right.

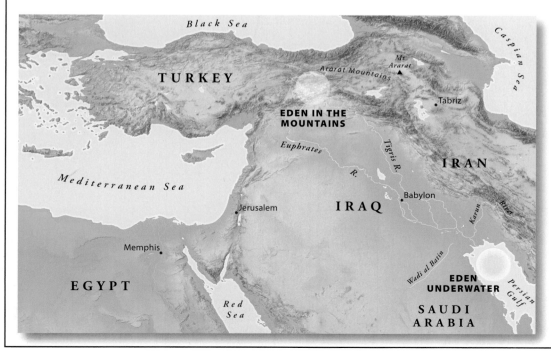

◄ IN SEARCH OF EDEN
One theory puts Eden in the mountains of northern Iran. Four rivers with names identical or similar to those in the Bible get their start in those mountains. Problem: other than mountain streams, there's no main river like the one the Bible says fed those four in Eden. A second theory puts Eden in what some say was once a river valley that flooded to become the Persian Gulf. Problem: all four rivers flow the wrong way—into Eden, instead of the direction the Bible says they flowed, out of Eden. Some wonder if this reversal was the writer's way of saying Eden can never be found.

▼ ARMED ANGEL To keep Adam and Eve from coming back to Eden, God stationed an armed guard on Eden's east border—a cherubim with a flaming sword. East of Iran's northern plains, where some say God planted the garden of Eden, there's a village called Helabad. Formerly known as Kheruabad, it was settled in ancient times by a tribe of fierce warriors called the Kheru. Some scholars say this could be a variation of *keruvim,* the Hebrew word for "cherubim."

◄ FIRST MENTION OF EDEN? The Bible isn't the first place to mention Eden, some scholars say. That distinction goes to this clay tablet with its wedge-shaped cuneiform letters pressed into soft clay a thousand years before Abraham from Sumer, the world's first known civilization. Sumerians lived in what is now Iraq. The word *edin,* meaning "plain," appears in one of their 5,000-year-old epics—the story Enmerkar and the Lord of Aratta. The story describes *edin* as a land of abundance.

Tabriz, where some say the garden of Eden was located, now covered in urban sprawl.

◄ FORBIDDEN APPLE? The Bible mentions apples several times, but not in the story of Adam and Eve. Some scholars suggest that a peach or an apricot was more likely Eve's dangling temptation. Yet apples were a favorite fruit in the ancient Middle East, and the prophet Joel said locusts destroyed apple orchards. Whatever the fruit, eating it brought death into the world. In an ancient Babylonian story, the plant was apparently seaweed. A warrior named Gilgamesh who lived about 5,000 years ago plucked a magical plant from the sea bottom. It was supposed to make him immortal—but a snake swallowed it.

ADAM FROM THE RED LAND

Red dirt is common in the Iranian mountains where some scholars speculate Eden once flourished. Adam sounds almost identical to words that mean "red" (*adom*), "dirt" (*adama*), and "blood" (*adamu*). The Bible plays off one of these connections by saying God made Adam from *adama.* An ancient burial custom in one of Iran's mountain villages seems to do much the same. When people died, their bodies were smeared with red dirt. Perhaps this symbolized that people were born and died covered in blood—or that they returned to the earth from which they came.

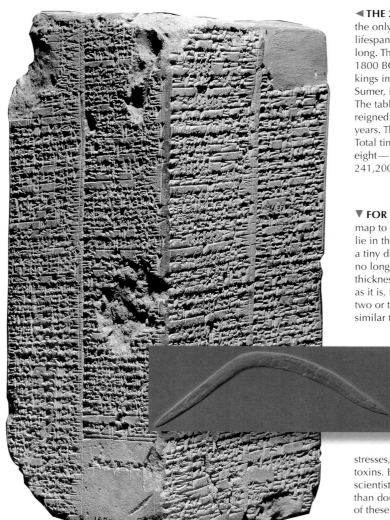

DID PEOPLE REALLY LIVE HUNDREDS OF YEARS?

Bible critics love this question.

After all, who in their right mind is going to believe that people once lived 900 years or more? Yet those are the kinds of numbers that show up in humanity's first family tree, preserved in Genesis 5.

It doesn't seem reasonable. If people lived as long as Methuselah—the Bible's eldest elder (age 969)—we might still be listening to Richard the Lion-heart tell war stories. Of the Crusades.

Many respected Bible scholars say they can't see any way of reading those numbers other than literally.

But some have tried finessing the math, saying the ancients measured time a different way—months as years, for example. That would help cut Mahalalel's age from 830 to a more believable 69. But it would also mean he fathered a son at age 5 instead of 65.

Others suggest that the lifespans didn't refer to individuals, but to their tribes. Yet that would mean God took Enoch's entire tribe away—letting them all escape death.

Still others have said the extreme numbers are symbolic. But if so, symbolic of what? No one has come up with a convincing answer.

In the absence of a reasonable explanation, many are left wondering if humanity's dwindling lifespan was the result of some physical change on the planet. Perhaps humanity was somehow poisoned by the forbidden fruit Adam and Eve ate. Or maybe the flood changed the environment in ways that tripped a chemical switch in the human body.

MOSES MAXED ▶

Moses lived 120 years, perhaps a symbol of what God set as the ceiling of human lifespan, the age God would allow humans to live after he saw how evil they had become (Genesis 6:3). In the next chapter of Genesis, God sent the great flood. The Bible says people before the flood lived hundreds of years. After the flood, humans began living about as long as we do today.

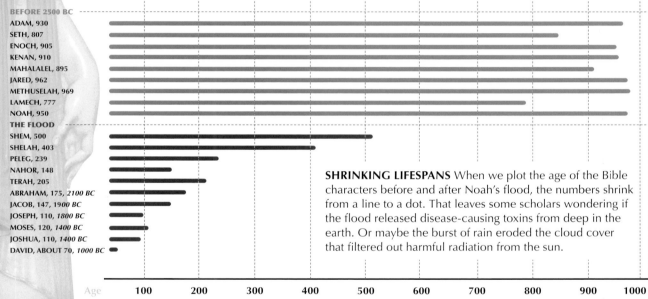

	BEFORE 2500 BC
ADAM, 930	
SETH, 807	
ENOCH, 905	
KENAN, 910	
MAHALALEL, 895	
JARED, 962	
METHUSELAH, 969	
LAMECH, 777	
NOAH, 950	
THE FLOOD	
SHEM, 500	
SHELAH, 403	
PELEG, 239	
NAHOR, 148	
TERAH, 205	
ABRAHAM, 175, *2100 BC*	
JACOB, 147, *1900 BC*	
JOSEPH, 110, *1800 BC*	
MOSES, 120, *1400 BC*	
JOSHUA, 110, *1400 BC*	
DAVID, ABOUT 70, *1000 BC*	

Age 100 200 300 400 500 600 700 800 900 1000

SHRINKING LIFESPANS When we plot the age of the Bible characters before and after Noah's flood, the numbers shrink from a line to a dot. That leaves some scholars wondering if the flood released disease-causing toxins from deep in the earth. Or maybe the burst of rain eroded the cloud cover that filtered out harmful radiation from the sun.

◀ **DID ANGELS MARRY WOMEN?** "The sons of God saw that the daughters of men were beautiful, and they married any of them they chose" (Genesis 6:2). Were these "sons of God" spirit beings, such as fallen angels or demons? That's what the oldest known theory says. It comes from Jewish scholars before the time of Christ. Though many scholars today agree, others argue that Jesus said angels don't marry (Mark 12:25). But perhaps Jesus was referring to angels in good standing. A second theory is that the sons of God were rulers and nobles—perhaps demon-possessed—who took into their harems any women they wanted. The Hebrew word for "god" (*elohim*) sometimes refers to leaders, such as judges (Exodus 22:8). Whoever or whatever the "sons of God" were, God's response was to declare that humans would live only 120 years.

WAS THERE REALLY A WORLDWIDE FLOOD?

Most geologists say there's no geological evidence to support the Bible's story that a flood covered the planet. They argue that seashells on mountaintops—sometimes used as evidence for a worldwide flood—simply proves what they teach in Geology 101: mountains start low and push their way up.

Many Christians, however, counter by saying geology's problem is its incorrect presumptions used to date the earth. These Christians—scientists among them—insist that the earth's layers were deposited rapidly by the flood.

One fact is not debatable.

Flood stories cover the entire world. From the Middle East to Ireland to the South Pacific, there are stories from nearly seventy cultures of a flood that decimated humanity.

How do experts explain all these stories, given the drought of geological proof?

There are two main theories, and you can find Christians who trust the Bible in both groups.

- The flood covered the entire world.
- The flood was regional, covering perhaps the civilized world or just one main population center.

Archaeologist C. Leonard Woolley captured headlines in 1929 when he announced he had found evidence of the flood. What he found was eight feet of silt sandwiched between two levels of occupation in the ancient riverfront city of Ur—cultural center of the world's first known civilization, Sumer. Abraham's hometown, Ur rested on the banks of the Euphrates River in southern Iraq. The estimated flood date was 6,000 to 7,500 years ago, more than 2,000 years before Abraham. Other river towns also showed signs of flooding, but the dates didn't match.

In 1998, geologists Walter Pitman and William Ryan said the flood stories might spring from a deluge about 7,500 years ago that turned a freshwater lake into the Black Sea. That's 200 miles north of the Ararat mountains where Noah's ark ran aground.

Whether Noah's flood covered the entire world or just an entire populated region, the mark it left on the human race is as obvious as a rainbow.

◄ Geologists theorize that melting ice from glaciers during the Ice Age raised the ocean. In time, the ocean's brim found a Bosporus gully and poured into it with a force many times greater than Niagara Falls, cutting what is now the half-mile- to three-mile-wide strait. Black Sea underwater studies by an exploration team partly funded by the National Geographic Society seem to confirm that the lake's shoreline rose 500 feet, pushing twenty miles inland.

◄ **BABYLON'S NOAH** Written centuries before Moses could have recorded Noah's story in Genesis, this clay tablet tells of a flood sent by Babylonian gods. One man and his family survived by building a cube-shaped boat and filling it with animals. Many parts of the story are strikingly similar to the Bible's version. In both accounts the boat came to rest on a mountain.

- Epic of Gilgamesh: "When the seventh day arrived, I sent out a dove. The dove went out, but came back. There was no resting place."

- Genesis 8:8 – 9: "Then he sent out a dove to see if the water had receded from the surface of the ground. But the dove could find no place to set its feet . . . so it returned."

▼ **FLOOD STORIES AROUND THE WORLD**
Zeus, chief god of the Greeks, was said to have destroyed the wicked human race with a flood. Only Deucalion and his wife Pyrrha survived, because they were good. Warned of the flood, this couple built a box-shaped boat that came to rest on a mountain. The Irish tell of Queen Cesair and her palace officials sailing for seven years after Ireland flooded. Tahitians tell of a sea god who got mad when a fisherman snagged a hook into his hair. He flooded all but the tops of the mountains.

▼ **FLOODING THE BLACK SEA** Noah's flood story, according to a new theory, may have come from the cataclysmic flood that geologists say turned a freshwater lake into the Black Sea. The photo here marks the breakthrough point—Turkey's Bosporus Strait, as seen from the space shuttle.

Black Sea

Bosporus Strait

Sea of Marmara

Ararat Mountains

Nineveh

IRAN

Euphrates R.

Tigris R.

IRAQ

Babylon

SUMER

Ur

SAUDI ARABIA

◄ **IN SEARCH OF THE FLOOD**
Noah's flood, some say, might have been limited to Iraq's river valley where civilization began, or to the Black Sea. Geologists confirm devastating ancient floods in both places. The Hebrew word for earth can also mean country or territory, reinforcing the theory of a regional flood instead of one that covered the earth.

Another argument is that the planet's water resources had to triple to cover the mountains. One counterpoint says not necessarily—today's towering mountains might have been created by the force of that flood.

WHATEVER HAPPENED TO NOAH'S ARK?

When the waters of the great flood receded, "the ark came to rest on the mountains of Ararat" (Genesis 8:4).

That's all the Bible says about it. We're left to wonder if Noah recycled the wood, or if he abandoned the ark.

The first person on record to report an ark sighting in the Ararat mountains was a Babylonian historian, Berossos, writing in the late 200s BC.

"It is said there is still some part of this ship in Armenia," Berossos wrote, "in the Gordyaean Mountains, and that some people carry off pieces of the bitumen." Bitumen is a waterproofing tar with which Noah coated the ark. Berossos said the people used the dried tar chunks as amulets to ward off evil.

In recent decades, explorers from the United States and other countries have targeted the highest mountain in the range and launched expeditions in the hopes of finding the ark.

So far there's no convincing evidence the ark landed there. Hand-tooled wood recovered from the mountain isn't nearly old enough to have been cut in Noah's day. Ark-shaped bumps photographed from planes, space shuttles, and satellites have turned out to be just that—bumps of rock and dirt. As for eyewitnesses who said they saw the ark, some have admitted to lying and others have failed to prove their claims.

► **NOAH'S BARGE** The ark looked more like a floating warehouse than a boat. At about 150 yards long and 25 yards wide, two arks could have parked side-by-side on a football field—though pushing through the end zone and past the sidelines. The ark stood 45 feet high, roughly the height of a four-story building. Some marine engineers say they doubt that a wooden ship this large could retain its shape in an ocean storm. Models of a wooden ark, however, have survived wave tank experiments.

► TIGHT PACK In the 1600s, Jesuit priest Athanasius Kircher created this floor plan to help prove that the world's animals would have fit on Noah's three-deck ark. Half the size of many cruise ships today, the ark had storage capacity about equal to 370 railroad boxcars. Some say that's enough room for two of each animal and the supplies they needed for the year they stayed on board—especially if Noah didn't have to take all 20,000 species or more of land animals. For example, some speculate he may have taken just the two dogs from which all other dogs came. Others say the ark's size was more appropriate for saving animals from a regional flood only.

► TIMBER ABOVE THE TIMBERLINE This chunk of hand-tooled wood is part of a five-foot-long beam that French explorer Fernand Navarra said he found in 1955 under a glacier on Mount Ararat. But the wood is only about 1,200 years old—nowhere close to the flood date sometime before 4,500 years ago. Many speculate that Noah's ark decayed, arguing that water starts the process by allowing fungus to grow and consume the wood. Others say glacial forces probably chewed the ark to shreds and spit the splinters down the mountain. Some, however, remain hopeful that pieces of Noah's ark remain buried somewhere in the snow.

IS NOAH'S ARK A SNOWBALL?

A picture of snowcapped Mount Ararat was snapped from a space shuttle 211 miles above the earth. The highest mountain in the Ararat range, this extinct volcano is where many speculate Noah's ark came to rest. Mount Ararat stands nearly 17,000 feet high to the northwest of Little Ararat at almost 13,000 feet. Turks call the dead volcano *Agri Dagi,* meaning Pain Mountain. Explorers have been climbing it for at least half a century, looking for the ark mainly in two areas: the Ahora Gorge that drops 6,000 feet from the summit, and the western plateau. These are where some eyewitnesses claim to have seen the ark, and where aerial and space photos have shown ark-sized shapes.

Mt. Ararat
Little Ararat

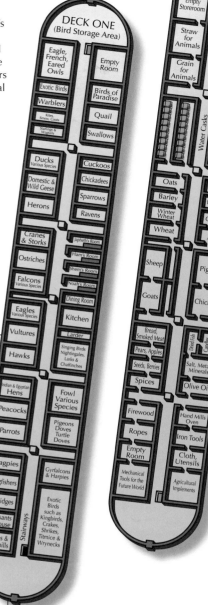

DECK ONE
(Bird Storage Area)

Eagle, French, Eared Owls | Empty Room
Exotic Birds | Birds of Paradise
Warblers | Quail
Kites, Smew, Coots |
Starlings & Wagtails | Swallows
Ducks Various Species | Cuckoos
Domestic & Wild Geese | Chickadees
Herons | Sparrows
| Ravens
Cranes & Storks | Japheth's Room
Ostriches | Ham's Room
Falcons Various Species | Shem's Room
| Noah's Room
Eagles Various Species | Dining Room
Vultures | Kitchen
Hawks | Larder
| Singing Birds Nightingales, Larks & Chaffinches
Indian & Egyptian Hens | Fowl Various Species
Peacocks | Pigeons Doves Turtle Doves
Parrots |
Magpies | Gyrfalcons & Harpies
Kingfishers |
Partridges | Exotic Birds such as Kingbirds, Crakes, Shrikes, Titmice & Wrynecks
Pheasants & Grouse |
Pelicans & Spoonbills | Stairways

DECK TWO
(Food Area)

Empty Storeroom | Cattle, Horses & Asses
Straw for Animals | Hay for Herbivores
Grain for Animals | Winter Fodder
Water Casks
Oats | Lentils, Rice
Barley | Beans, Peas
Winter Wheat | Chestnuts
Wheat | Nuts, Acorns
Sheep | Pigeons
Goats | Chickens
Bread, Smoked Meat | Dried Fish | Candles, Honey
Pears, Apples | Salt, Metal, Minerals
Seeds, Berries | Olive Oil
Spices |
Firewood | Hand Mills Oven
Ropes | Iron Tools
Empty Room | Cloth, Utensils
Mechanical Tools for the Future World | Agricultural Implements

DECK THREE
(Animal Area)

Cistern | Empty Storeroom
| Badgers
Boars, Pigs | Porcupines
Foxes | Tortoises
Wolves | Seals
Lynxes | Indian Dogs
Unicorns | Maltese
Panthers | Purebreeds
Tigers | Greyhounds
| Retrievers
Bears | Chamois
Lions | Reindeer
Rhinos | Deer
Elephants | Cattle
Camels | Goats
Dromedaries | Sheep
Horses | Bison
Asses | Elk
Onagers | Gazelles
Cats | Bushbucks
Monkeys | Hippos
Rabbits | Crocodiles
Squirrels | Otters
Indian Pigs | Beavers
Conies |
Empty Room |
| Cistern

► DINOSAURS, TOO? Look close and you'll see dinosaurs joining the march into Noah's ark. Christians who say the earth is just a few thousand years old argue that dinosaurs and people coexisted. Many Christians disagree, however, insisting that scientific techniques such as carbon dating don't support the young earth theory.

WHAT WAS THE TOWER OF BABEL?

Noah's descendants settled in a fertile plain, perhaps along a river in what is now Iraq. They said, "Come, let us build ourselves a city, with a tower that reaches to the heavens, so that we may make a name for ourselves and not be scattered over the face of the whole earth" (Genesis 11:4).

Most scholars agree that the tower was likely a stair-step pyramid called a ziggurat, which dominated city skylines at the time. Ruins of about thirty have been found so far.

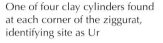

One of four clay cylinders found at each corner of the ziggurat, identifying site as Ur

Ziggurats weren't usually treated as temples, but as stairways to the sky. The temple generally stood next door. It seems ziggurats were intended to make it easy for the gods to come down and help the people, and for religious leaders to go up and talk to the gods.

Everyone spoke the same language, the Bible says. God brought the project to a halt when he made the people speak in different languages. Confused, they abandoned their work and scattered abroad by language groups.

One story from Sumer reports that all people once spoke Sumerian. At least they did until an angry god introduced other languages. The leader of the gods, Enki, "changed the speech in their mouths, bringing confusion into it—into the speech that until then had been one" (*Enmerkar and the Lord of Aratta*).

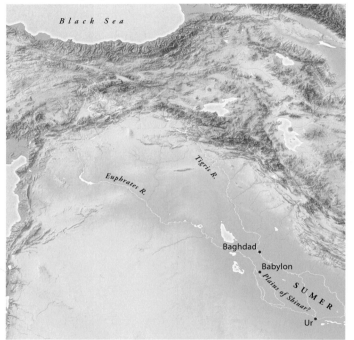

◀ **NO X MARKS THE SPOT** Somewhere on the plains of Shinar, Noah's descendants built the Tower of Babel. Shinar's exact location remains a mystery, but many scholars point to the birthplace of Middle Eastern civilization: the plain between the Tigris and Euphrates rivers in what is now Iraq. Some say Shinar may be an early form of Sumer, the name of the world's first known empire.

▶ **TOWER IN ABRAHAM'S HOMETOWN** The tower of Babel may have been a ziggurat, much like this one in Abraham's hometown of Ur—the New York City of its day. In this artist's reconstruction of a New Year's processional, worshipers carry a statue of their moon god to the tower top. Ziggurats were considered stairways to heaven.

◀ **ONE BRICK AT A TIME** Like this reconstructed wall in the ruins of ancient Babylon, the Tower of Babel was built of mud bricks. Though stones were the strongest building material in Bible times, there weren't many in the region. So builders strengthened mud bricks by baking them in kilns—a process that developed in the 3000s BC. For mortar, builders used asphalt-like tar from tar pits, which waterproofed the bricks.

▲ **ARTISTIC LICENSE** After visiting Italy, Flemish artist Pieter Bruegel in 1563 pictured the Tower of Babel as looking a bit like Italy's Leaning Tower of Pisa, built 400 years earlier.

BABYLON'S TOWER OF BABEL

South Baghdad may once have been home to the Tower of Babel. That's where ancient Babylon stood—a city the Israelites called Babel. Dominating Babylon's flat-roofed skyline is a seven-level ziggurat that rose about 300 feet high, an estimate based on the foundation's dimensions. The ziggurat walls have long since been carried off—one sturdy brick at a time—as locals recycled them.

WHY CIRCUMCISION AS A SYMBOL OF GOD'S PROMISE TO ABRAHAM?

Abraham was ninety-nine years old when God promised to make him the father of nations. But Abraham had to obey the terms of an agreement with God. This was essentially a contract—a covenant. Abraham had to cut off his foreskin and the foreskin of every male in his household. In addition, future generations had to circumcise eight-day-old boys. This kept the covenant alive from one generation to the next. God warned that any uncircumcised male "will be cut off from his people; he has broken my covenant" (Genesis 17:14).

The Bible never explains why God chose circumcision. But even in ancient times, scholars offered guesses. Josephus, a Jewish historian in the first century, said it was to keep Jewish "posterity unmixed with others."

Many scholars today say he was wrong.

Circumcision had nothing to do with racial purity. God told Abraham and his descendants to circumcise Hebrews and non-Hebrews alike—whoever chose to serve God. Circumcision welcomed them into the covenant filled with blessings.

Many of Israel's neighbors circumcised their boys. Canaanites did. Arabs circumcised boys as a coming of age ritual at thirteen, when Abraham's son Ishmael—father of the Arabs—was circumcised. Hittites circumcised their seven-day-old boys. Egyptians slit the top of the foreskin and let it hang free.

What was unique about Hebrew circumcision was that God took this common Middle Eastern practice and gave it spiritual meaning.

▼ **THE SIGN OF GOD'S COVENANT**
Abraham obeys God and circumcises all the males in his family, including servants. No one knows how circumcision began, since it was practiced centuries before Abraham. Some speculate it was originally a fertility ritual conducted before marriage. Or perhaps it signified that a boy had become a man. Or maybe it was to appease an angry god. For the people of Israel, however, it was simply a command of God that they chose to obey.

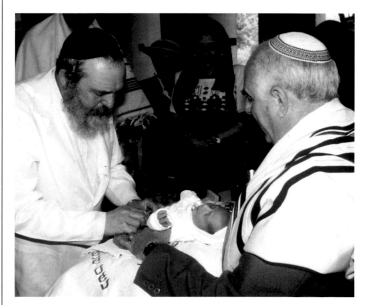

◄ **A JOYFUL FAMILY OCCASION**
On the eighth day of his life, a Jewish boy is circumcised and given his Hebrew name. The ceremony marks him as someone who's included in the covenant between Abraham's descendents and God. The occasion is so important that Jews are permitted to conduct the ritual not only on the Sabbath but even on the holiest day of the year—the day of repentance called Yom Kippur.

◄ **AN ANGRY CIRCUMCISION** Bible experts are puzzled about why the wife of Moses hastily circumcised her son, smeared the blood on Moses, and complained, "Surely you are a bridegroom of blood to me," (Exodus 4:25). The family was on its way to Egypt to free the Hebrews when God revealed he was about to kill Moses or the boy—scholars aren't sure which. Perhaps God was angry at Moses for not circumcising the boy sooner. Or maybe God wanted the boy protected from the tenth plague that would claim the life of the oldest non-Hebrew child in each family.

◄ **JEWISH AND ASHAMED** Nudity was common in Greek and Roman times. Athletes competed in the nude and many people bathed in public facilities. Greeks and Romans were disgusted by Jewish circumcision, which they considered self-mutilation and indecent. The head of the penis, they believed, should be kept covered. Because of the ridicule, many Jews abandoned circumcision, or compromised by cutting away only part of the skin.

► **TOOLS OF CIRCUMCISION** Ritual implements include a knife and a thin metal shield. The foreskin is slipped through the shield which protects the head of the penis and serves as a guide for the blade.

A WORD TO CRITICS

To defend circumcision, Jewish philosopher Philo, who lived in the time of Christ, offered six explanations. Three were practical: circumcision makes it easier to stay clean; prevents infection and disease; and makes it easier to have children because semen doesn't get trapped in the folds of foreskin. Three were philosophical: circumcision symbolizes a connection between our thought life and our physical life because the head of a circumcised penis (physical life) resembles the heart (thought life); symbolizes cutting away lustful obsessions "that delude the mind"; and symbolizes the removing of evil from our hearts.

WHAT HAPPENED TO SODOM AND GOMORRAH?

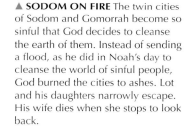

"The LORD rained down burning sulfur on Sodom and Gomorrah . . . Lot's wife looked back, and she became a pillar of salt" (Genesis 19:24, 26).

Two theories about how this happened seem to track with what geologists say about the Dead Sea region, where Bible scholars say the twin cities were likely located.

Theory 1. Two plates of the earth's crust located on both sides of the Dead Sea slipped, producing an earthquake. This land is rich in minerals—sulfur, salt, oil, and pockets of natural gas. Lightning or a fire ignited the gas, showering the entire plain with burning minerals. Lot's wife, who paused to look, may have gotten caught in the spray.

Theory 2. The cities were built on sandy soil near the Dead Sea. An earthquake momentarily caused the sand to float in the water beneath it—becoming like quicksand. Retired geologist Graham M. Harris wrote in the *Quarterly Journal of Engineering Geology* that this kind of "liquefaction" could explain how Sodom and Gomorrah were destroyed. As the cities collapsed, fires that had been lit in the early dawn of a new day—when the Bible says God destroyed the cities—may have ignited natural gas or oil.

A geologist from the British Museum along with geologists from Cambridge and Hull universities in England tested Harris's idea of liquefaction with a scale model. During a simulated earthquake at a magnitude of six, the model not only collapsed, it slid with the slope of the land. That means Sodom and Gomorrah may have slid right into the Dead Sea—with a little nudge from the finger of God.

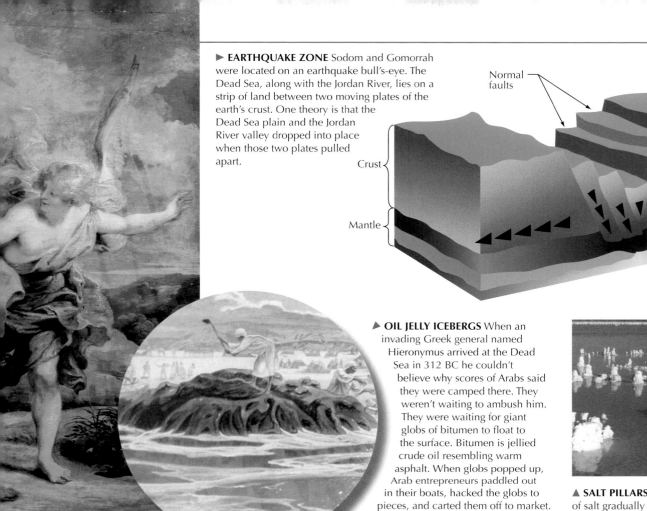

▶ **EARTHQUAKE ZONE** Sodom and Gomorrah were located on an earthquake bull's-eye. The Dead Sea, along with the Jordan River, lies on a strip of land between two moving plates of the earth's crust. One theory is that the Dead Sea plain and the Jordan River valley dropped into place when those two plates pulled apart.

Normal faults

Crust

Mantle

▶ **OIL JELLY ICEBERGS** When an invading Greek general named Hieronymus arrived at the Dead Sea in 312 BC he couldn't believe why scores of Arabs said they were camped there. They weren't waiting to ambush him. They were waiting for giant globs of bitumen to float to the surface. Bitumen is jellied crude oil resembling warm asphalt. When globs popped up, Arab entrepreneurs paddled out in their boats, hacked the globs to pieces, and carted them off to market. Customers used it as waterproof caulk for their boats, as mortar to hold brick homes together, and even as a laxative. Egyptians bought it as a cheap substitute for the sweet-smelling plant sap they stuffed inside mummies.

▲ **SALT PILLARS** Crusty islands of salt gradually form salt pillars in the shallow water at the Dead Sea's southern end. The Dead Sea is 25 percent salt—four times saltier than the ocean.

DEAD TOWNS BY DEAD SEA

Sodom and Gomorrah might be among the ruins of five cities discovered along the south shore of the Dead Sea. Bab edh-Dhra is the largest, and may have been Sodom—which seems to have been the dominate city of what the Bible calls five "cities of the plain." Eight miles south is Numeira, possibly Gomorrah. Both cities were destroyed by fire around the time of Abraham and Lot, some 4,000 years ago. Numeria, better preserved, was covered by a layer of ash more than a foot thick in places. Some theories place Sodom and Gomorrah underwater, near a ridge called Mount Sodom. Others place them in the Jordan River valley above the Dead Sea because it's a fertile area. But some speculate that the now-barren plains south of the Dead Sea were once fertile.

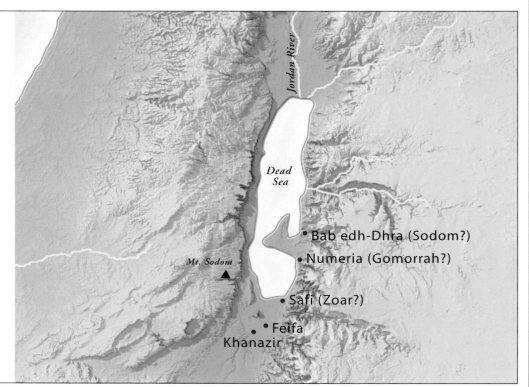

Jordan River

Dead Sea

Mt. Sodom ▲

• Bab edh-Dhra (Sodom?)

• Numeria (Gomorrah?)

• Safi (Zoar?)

• Feifa
Khanazir

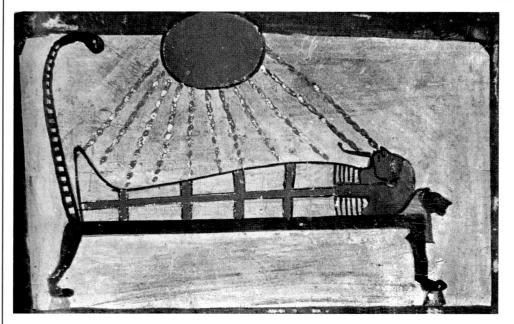

WERE THE PLAGUES OF EGYPT NATURAL DISASTERS?

Egyptian king Akhenaton offers a sacrifice to the sun god, ca. 1350 BC.

It's possible, some Bible scholars and scientists agree, that most of Egypt's ten plagues followed a seasonal cycle of natural disasters—starting with autumn floods and ending with crop ruin the next spring. Like a row of falling dominoes, each disaster triggered the next.

1. Nile River turned blood red, killing the fish. Egyptians depended on moderate annual flooding to irrigate the farmland and lay down a fresh coat of topsoil. On rare occasions, poisonous organisms from decaying algae in the swamplands upriver got washed into the floodwater. Some dying algae, such as *Trichodesmus,* turn the water red. That's where the nearby Red Sea gets its name.

2. Frog invasion. Fleeing the flood, frogs died in heaps, perhaps from the same toxin that killed the fish.

3. Swarms of flying insects. These might be gnats, mosquitoes, or some other insects that breed in pools of receding floodwater.

4. Swarms of flies. A single stable fly—common in Egypt—lays hundreds of eggs in wet and decaying places such as soaked straw or dead frogs.

5. Diseased livestock. Anthrax is one of many possibilities, since it can be transmitted through contaminated drinking water.

6. Boils on humans and livestock. A stable fly can produce blisters. So can anthrax, which moves up the food chain as people eat diseased animals.

7. Hail. It destroyed the flax and barley crops, which grow over the winter. Harvest begins around February.

8. Locusts. Pesticides control them today. More than half a million acres were treated in the region for a 1998 infestation.

9. Darkness for three days. A blinding sandstorm that Egyptians call Khamsin, meaning "fifty days," can blast in from the Sahara anytime from March through May, forcing drivers today to use their headlights.

10. Death of oldest child. This plague doesn't seem to fit the pattern. Some scholars say that the oldest child was typically pampered, and given bigger servings of food. And if the food was contaminated—by locust droppings, for example—the oldest children would have gotten sickest. But first-born animals died too.

The Bible doesn't say if the plagues were natural disasters. But Moses made one thing clear to Pharaoh: God was behind them, "so you may know that the earth is the LORD's" (Exodus 9:29).

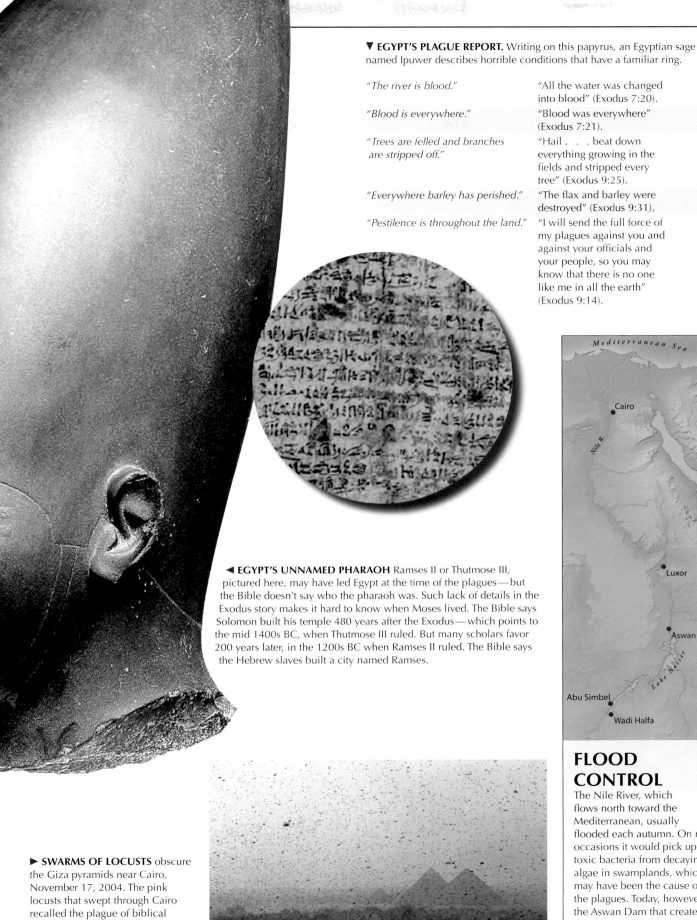

▼ **EGYPT'S PLAGUE REPORT.** Writing on this papyrus, an Egyptian sage named Ipuwer describes horrible conditions that have a familiar ring.

"The river is blood."	"All the water was changed into blood" (Exodus 7:20).
"Blood is everywhere."	"Blood was everywhere" (Exodus 7:21).
"Trees are felled and branches are stripped off."	"Hail . . . beat down everything growing in the fields and stripped every tree" (Exodus 9:25).
"Everywhere barley has perished."	"The flax and barley were destroyed" (Exodus 9:31).
"Pestilence is throughout the land."	"I will send the full force of my plagues against you and against your officials and your people, so you may know that there is no one like me in all the earth" (Exodus 9:14).

◄ **EGYPT'S UNNAMED PHARAOH** Ramses II or Thutmose III, pictured here, may have led Egypt at the time of the plagues—but the Bible doesn't say who the pharaoh was. Such lack of details in the Exodus story makes it hard to know when Moses lived. The Bible says Solomon built his temple 480 years after the Exodus—which points to the mid 1400s BC, when Thutmose III ruled. But many scholars favor 200 years later, in the 1200s BC when Ramses II ruled. The Bible says the Hebrew slaves built a city named Ramses.

Mediterranean Sea

Cairo

Nile R.

Luxor

Aswan

Lake Nasser

Abu Simbel

Wadi Halfa

FLOOD CONTROL

The Nile River, which flows north toward the Mediterranean, usually flooded each autumn. On rare occasions it would pick up toxic bacteria from decaying algae in swamplands, which may have been the cause of the plagues. Today, however, the Aswan Dam that created Lake Nasser in 1970 helps control flooding.

► **SWARMS OF LOCUSTS** obscure the Giza pyramids near Cairo, November 17, 2004. The pink locusts that swept through Cairo recalled the plague of biblical Egypt, flying high above tall towers and scaring pedestrians who stamped on them or ran for cover.

HOW LARGE WAS THE EXODUS CROWD?

The Bible is all too clear about how many people Moses led through the Martian-like badlands of the Sinai Peninsula, on the trek up to the Promised Land.

Here's the problem: the numbers are astronomical.

"There were about six hundred thousand men on foot, besides women and children" (Exodus 12:37). Wives and kids could have pushed the refugee population to two or three million.

That's the population of Chicago. On the move. In a water-starved land.

If this swath of humanity lined up to cross the Red Sea in rows 100 yards wide, the front row would have marched some twenty miles ahead of the dust-chewers in the back.

What are we to make of this?

Many Bible students take the numbers literally, trusting that the God who hung the stars in the sky is fully capable of dealing with astronomical numbers.

Others search for explanations they can grasp. Among the many theories, two are especially intriguing.

WRONG WORD The Hebrew word *elep* usually means "thousands." But sometimes it means "clans." These are extended families: fathers with the families of their married sons. If that's what it meant here, perhaps there were just 600 clans. Moses may have led 20,000 Hebrews—or fewer.

NUMBERED ALPHABET Hebrew letters have numerical equivalents (as in A=1, B=2). The census Moses took tallied 603,551 men. That's just one number above the sum of Hebrew letters spelling out "sons of Israel"—603,550. Perhaps the writer's point was that Moses led out all the Hebrews—however many there were.

◄ **"ISRAEL IS WIPED OUT"** History's first mention of Israel reports the Hebrew people exterminated. This seven-feet-high black granite slab honoring the memory of Pharaoh Merenptah—successor of Ramses the Great—says "Israel is laid waste, its seed is not." Erected in Thebes around 1207 BC, this monument seems to argue against scholars who say the Hebrews arrived in Israel just a few decades earlier. It probably would have taken more than a few decades for Egypt to consider Israel an independent nation. Even so, many scholars say evidence of destroyed cities in Israel points to an exodus date in the mid–1200s rather than the date suggested by a literal reading of Scripture—the mid–1400s. First Kings 6:1 says the exodus occurred 480 years before Solomon built the temple—estimated at about 966 BC. If this interpretation is right, Moses led the Hebrews out of Egypt in 1446 BC. But some wonder if the 480 years is another way of saying a dozen generations, with each generation rounded off to forty years. Scholars are still debating the numbers.

◀ **BUILDER KING** Ramses the Great was known for his massive building projects—including entire cities. Hebrews built Pithom and Ramses, the Bible says. For this reason, some argue that the exodus couldn't have been before the 1200s BC, when Ramses ruled. But both cities existed in the 1400s BC. Ramses apparently renovated and renamed them. The writer of Exodus may have called the cities by their newer, more familiar names, even though the Hebrews built the earlier cities.

A GENERATION'S OASIS.

Moses and the Hebrews spent about forty years at Kadesh Barnea, an oasis on Egypt's side of the Egypt-Israeli border. Exactly which oasis is uncertain, but most scholars guess it was Ein el-Qudeirat, an oasis with the largest spring in the northern Sinai. This spring produces more than 10,000 gallons of water an hour—a quarter of a million a day. If there were two million Hebrews, as some estimate, this spring would have provided each person with only two cups of water a day—not nearly enough for them and their herds in this hot and rocky wasteland. But it would have easily sustained 20,000 or more refugees and their herds.

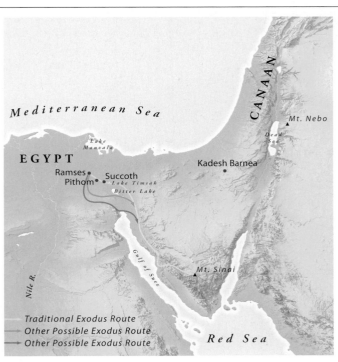

Mediterranean Sea

CANAAN

EGYPT

Lake Manzala

Mt. Nebo

Dead Sea

Kadesh Barnea

Ramses
Pithom • Succoth
Lake Timsah
Bitter Lake

Nile R.

Gulf of Suez

Mt. Sinai

→ Traditional Exodus Route
→ Other Possible Exodus Route
→ Other Possible Exodus Route

Red Sea

▼ **A SWARM OF HEBREWS** Bible experts are uncertain how many Hebrews Moses led out of Egypt. One argument for accepting the Bible's report of incredibly high numbers is because the Hebrew language describes them as "a swarm." Their numbers grew so high that Egyptian leaders worried the foreigners might take over. So they enslaved them and took desperate stabs at population control: working them to death and killing newborn males.

DID THE RED SEA REALLY PART?

Trapped between the sea and the Egyptian chariot corps, the fleeing Hebrews witnessed what is perhaps the most famous miracle of all—a miracle the Bible talks about more than any other.

"Moses stretched out his hand over the sea, and all that night the LORD drove the sea back with a strong east wind and turned it into dry land. The waters were divided" (Exodus 14: 21).

The Bible doesn't say where this happened or exactly how. Experts in various fields of study offer theories.

WHERE Some speculate the northern tip of the Gulf of Suez, where the water is shallow enough to be pushed around by strong winds but deep enough to drown people. Others say it was more likely in one of the marshy lakes to the north—such as Bitter Lakes or Lake Timsah. That's because the Hebrew words often translated Red Sea, *yam suf*, more likely mean Sea of Reeds, since *suf* appears to come from the Egyptian word for reeds that grew along the banks of freshwater lakes and rivers.

HOW Some argue for a tidal wave churned up by an earthquake, since this region sits above a massive rip in the earth's crust. An earthquake could have spawned an ocean tidal wave that pulled water from the shoreline—mimicking an excessively low tide—and then built the water into a huge wave that broke on top of the Egyptians as they chased the Hebrews. Others say a strong wind blowing all night could have produced something similar—pushing the water nearly a mile out to sea before releasing it to rush back when the wind died.

▲ **MOSES WAS HERE?** Two Russian scientists in 2004 studied a four-mile-long reef running across the north end of the Gulf of Suez called Pharaoh's Bath. In a report published in the *Bulletin of the Russian Academy of Sciences,* they said that a strong wind blowing all night could have dried the reef of its ten-foot-deep water. When the wind let up, they said, the water would have rushed back in place within half an hour.

◄ **NAPOLEON'S RED SEA CROSSING** When Napoleon invaded Egypt in 1799, he nearly drowned when receded water from the Red Sea rushed back to shore with shocking speed. French accounts tell of him, on horseback, skillfully making his way back to shore. An Egyptian version has him falling off his horse and getting fished out of the water moments before drowning.

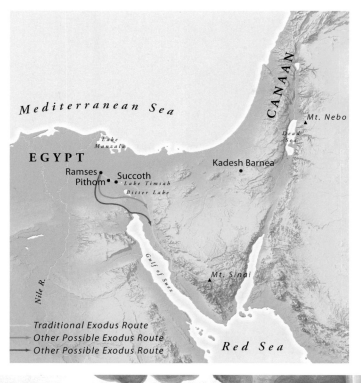

Traditional Exodus Route
Other Possible Exodus Route
Other Possible Exodus Route

◄ FOOTSTEPS OF MOSES

Released by Pharaoh, Moses and the Hebrews flee the Nile delta. They don't take the shortest route to what is now Israel—along the seacoast. Instead they bypass Egyptian outposts on that heavily traveled road, turning south into the Sinai Desert. Pharaoh decides he shouldn't have freed them, so he sends his chariot corps to bring them back. After just a few days of freedom, the Hebrews find themselves blocked by a large body of water—perhaps the Red Sea's Gulf of Suez or a lake to the north.

◄ PHARAOH'S WEATHER MIRACLE

Ramses II, the pharaoh many believe Moses had to deal with, once prayed to the god Seth for good weather. Ramses was worried about a Hittite princess traveling through the Turkish mountains in winter, on her way to marry him. "The sky is in your hands," he prayed. "May you not send rain, ice, or snow until the wonder you have planned for me arrives." Seth complied, the report says, keeping the winter skies as calm as summer.

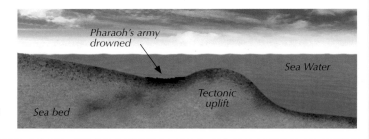

◄

PARTING THE WATER

A hot east wind rushes in from the Arabian Desert and blows all night, cutting a path through the sea. Though scientists say it's possible for wind to push back the shoreline, there's no clear explanation for the "wall of water on their right and on their left" (Exodus 14:22).

► **SCIENTIFIC THEORY** Because of the narrow, finger-like shape of the Gulf of Suez, a moderate wind of about forty-five miles per hour blowing for ten hours could push water back from shore nearly a mile. So says oceanographer Doron Nof of Florida State University and meteorologist Nathan Paldor of Jerusalem's Hebrew University, writing in the *Bulletin of the American Meteorological Society*. If there had been an underwater sandbar ridge at the time, Moses and the Hebrews could have walked on it, past water on both sides of them. Once the wind stopped, the scientists say, the water would have crashed back to shore.

Pharaoh's army drowned

Sea Water

Tectonic uplift

Sea bed

WHY DID THE ISRAELITES WORSHIP A GOLDEN CALF?

By the time the Hebrews pitched camp at Mount Sinai, they had seen many of God's remarkable miracles. They witnessed the ten plagues that prodded Pharaoh to free them. They watched in awe as the sea opened an escape route for them. And they saw the sea walls collapse just in time to drown the Egyptian chariot corps chasing them down.

After seeing all this with their own eyes, why would they be worried about Moses taking a long time to meet with God on Mount Sinai? So worried that they built a golden calf, "bowed down to it and sacrificed to it" (Exodus 32:8)?

The Bible doesn't say. So scholars offer theories. The calf represented

- God himself, since a young bull symbolized strength

- a local god, from Egypt or Canaan
- the moon god, Sin, from the homeland of their founding father Abraham, in what is now Iraq. Even the name "Sinai" may come from this god.

Whatever the calf represented, God was so angry about what the Hebrews had done that he offered to kill them and start fresh with Moses, as God had done earlier with Noah. Moses declined. But he too was angry enough that he executed the leaders.

Because the entire story spins around the anger of God and Moses, many Bible experts say the Hebrews probably broke the first and most important of the Ten Commandments. They worshipped the golden calf as a god.

◄ **MOSES WITH HORNS** Moses has horns in many paintings and statues, as he does in this statue located in Rome. The bizarre idea comes from an ancient Latin translation of the Bible—the Vulgate—which said that after meeting God, the face of Moses "became horned" (Exodus 34:29). Later translations said his face became radiant. Because of the mistranslation, some early Christian scholars suggested that the golden calf—horned—represented Moses.

◀ **MOUNTAIN OF MOSES** That's what this granite mountain is called by locals—*Jebel Musa* in Arabic. But it's more widely known as Mount Sinai—the place where Moses encountered God in a burning bush and later received the Ten Commandments. The Hebrews worshiped the golden calf at the base of Mount Sinai while waiting for Moses to return from meeting with God. A monastery now marks the site.

◀ **BULL RIDING WITH NO HANDS** A rain god wielding thunderbolts stands on his pedestal—a bull, which symbolizes the god's strength and virility. Images like this, common in the ancient Middle East, are why some scholars say the Israelites weren't actually worshiping the golden calf. Instead, they were honoring God by building him a stand. God, however, was not impressed. Other scholars say it's more likely the calf represented a god: Apis from Egypt, or El from what is now Israel, or perhaps Sin from Iraq.

◀ **BABYLON'S 282 COMMANDMENTS** The Ten Commandments Moses carried down from Mount Sinai wasn't the first set of laws etched in stone. Several hundred years earlier, Babylonian king Hammurabi had his kingdom's 282 laws inscribed onto an eight-foot-high black stone pillar. Some laws are similar to those Moses later taught the Israelites. "Eye for an eye, tooth for a tooth" (Exodus 21:24) condenses what by then was probably a well established law in the Middle East: "If a man puts out the eye of another man, his eye shall be put out. . . . If a man knocks out the teeth of his equal, his teeth shall be knocked out" (Hammurabi laws 196, 200).

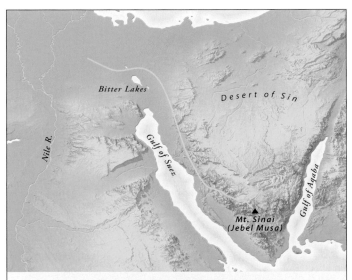

LOOKING FOR MOUNT SINAI

Moses may have taken his people to Israel by the not-so-scenic route: the Martian-like badlands of southern Sinai. By going this way, they avoided the Egyptian outposts along the more heavily traveled routes in the north. The Bible doesn't say where Mount Sinai was, but tradition points to the 7,500-foot-high peak that towers over others in the south Sinai range. Christians memorialized this tradition by building a monastery there in the fourth century, shortly after Rome legalized Christianity.

▲ SACRIFICES FOR ALL OCCASIONS Jews offered so many kinds of sacrifices that it takes the first seven chapters of Leviticus to detail each one. Among the many sacrifices were those to atone for a sin, crown a king, celebrate a religious hozliday, and purify a woman after her monthly period. Most common was a burnt offering, in which an entire animal—such as a bird, lamb, or bull—was burned on the altar. With some sacrifices, the meat was divided among priest, worshiper, and God—with God's share burned to produce "an aroma pleasing to the LORD" (Leviticus 1:9). Not all sacrifices involved blood. Grain offerings apparently reminded people that God deserved thanks for the harvest.

WHY DID GOD REQUIRE BLOOD SACRIFICES?

It's hard for many to understand why the bond between God and human beings had to be sealed in blood. Even Jews—a people who sacrificed animals for 2,000 years—wonder why God required such a violent and expensive manner of worship. Killing animals was the main way Jews worshiped God from the time Abraham fathered their nation until the Romans tore down their only authorized place of sacrifice, the Jewish temple, in AD 70.

The Bible gives only a brief and puzzling explanation for blood sacrifices: "The life of a creature is in the blood, and I have given it to you to make atonement for yourselves on the altar; it is the blood that makes atonement for one's life" (Leviticus 17:11). Sin warrants the death penalty, but God allows the sacrifice of animals as a substitute to atone for sin.

"Atonement" refers to forgiveness. Scholars use a play on words to explain that "atonement" makes us "at one" with God—in a close relationship. Through these sacrifices, people sought forgiveness and expressed devotion.

But why blood?

Perhaps because blood serves as a graphic reminder of how serious sin is—serious enough that it brought death into the world. Also, it could be that God chose this worship practice partly because it was already common throughout the region by the time Moses delivered the many sacrificial laws. Animal sacrifice had a long tradition that went back to the first empire: Sumeria, in what is now Iraq. The Bible adds that Adam and Eve's son Abel was the first human to sacrifice animals to God.

GIVING TO GET

Sir Edward Tylor, first professor of anthropology for the University of Oxford, caused a stir when in the late 1800s he said that sacrifices started because people thought that by offering gifts to gods they would get something in return. Later anthropologists countered by explaining that sacrifices provided a link between gods and humanity. They said that's because people believed the sacrifice belonged to two worlds: its body belonged to the physical, and its life belonged to the spiritual. Some theologians see Jesus in this description—the perfect link between God and humanity.

▶ CONTINUING THE TRADITION Though Jews stopped sacrificing animals in AD 70 when Rome tore down the Jerusalem temple, Samaritans still offer sacrifices. Samaritans had previously broken away from the Jewish faith and worshiped God in the hills of central Israel. Today, this surviving community of several hundred Samaritans sacrifices Passover offerings on Mount Gerizim, about thirty miles north of Jerusalem.

▼ THE FIRST ANIMAL SACRIFICE Animals have been killed for the sins of humanity since the very beginning. Surprisingly, it seems God was the first to sacrifice animals. After Adam and Eve sinned and wanted to hide their nakedness, "God made garments of skin for Adam and his wife" (Genesis 3:21).

▲ SACRIFICE TO END ALL SACRIFICES New Testament writers said the Jewish law—including laws about sacrifice—were just shadows of what God one day planned to do for his people. Jesus is presented as "the Lamb of God, who takes away the sin of the world" (John 1:29). Unlike sacrifices the Jewish people had to offer continually, Jesus "sacrificed for their sins once for all when he offered himself" (Hebrews 7:27).

▲ JEWISH ALTAR Jews burned their animal sacrifices on altars like this one found at Beersheba, distinguished by four corner projections called horns. Perhaps the horns helped hold the wood or meat in place. During some sacrifices, the priest would collect part of the animal's blood and splash it on the horns and the base of the altar—perhaps symbolizing the altar purified from top to bottom.

29

WHY KOSHER FOOD?

Jews can eat crickets and grasshoppers but not pork or lobster.

It sounds like a mean joke, yet the menu Moses delivered to the Israelites more than 3,000 years ago includes hopping insects, while excluding some of the tastier delights in the animal kingdom. His instructions outlined exactly what animals the people of Israel could eat.

On land: animals that have a split hoof and chew the cud—with a cud being a wad of food they chew, swallow, and bring back up to chew again.

In the sea: only fish that have scales and fins.

In the air: there's no general rule—just a list of birds scratched from the menu.

Scholars in various fields—from biology to theology—have tried to find a pattern in these food restrictions. You could fill your plate with the theories.

One theory says animals considered kosher—a Hebrew word meaning proper—were healthiest to eat.

Another says kosher animals were "normal." Nonkosher rejects were unusual in some way: fish without scales or birds that ate flesh.

Yet another says the Israelites ate what God symbolically ate. In other words, the most common animals they offered to God in sacrifices—cattle, sheep, and goats—were animals the people of Israel ate. But what about the kosher cricket?

That's the problem with these and other theories—some animals don't fit.

God didn't give any reason for the food restrictions. He simply said, "Do not defile yourselves by any of these creatures. . . . I am the LORD your God; consecrate yourselves and be holy, because I am holy" (Leviticus 11:43 – 44). So the Jews obeyed.

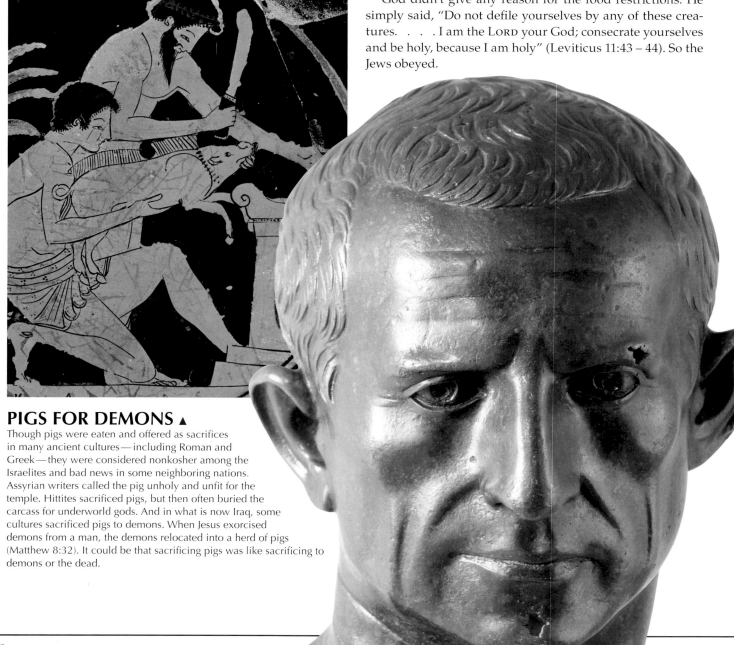

PIGS FOR DEMONS ▲

Though pigs were eaten and offered as sacrifices in many ancient cultures—including Roman and Greek—they were considered nonkosher among the Israelites and bad news in some neighboring nations. Assyrian writers called the pig unholy and unfit for the temple. Hittites sacrificed pigs, but then often buried the carcass for underworld gods. And in what is now Iraq, some cultures sacrificed pigs to demons. When Jesus exorcised demons from a man, the demons relocated into a herd of pigs (Matthew 8:32). It could be that sacrificing pigs was like sacrificing to demons or the dead.

EAT	DON'T EAT
Cows	Pork
Sheep	Rabbit
Goats	Bear
Grasshoppers	Camels
Crickets	Dogs
Locust	Buzzards
Quail	Eagles
Dove	Catfish
Pigeon	Lobster
Fish with scales and fins	Shrimp

▲ **KEEPING IT KOSHER** Even kosher meat can become nonkosher if improperly prepared. The butchering is carefully monitored. The knife that slits an animal's throat is inspected to make sure it's razor sharp. Organs of the animal are inspected for signs of disease that would render the meat unfit. The carcass is hung upside-down to drain out the blood. "Be sure you do not eat the blood, because the blood is the life, and you must not eat the life with the meat" (Deuteronomy 12:23). Blood, a symbol of the life God gives, belonged to God. In ancient sacrifice rituals, Jewish priests caught some of the blood and splashed it on the altar.

THE END OF KOSHER

With a single sentence, Jesus rattled Jewish leaders by giving notice that the thousand-year-old food laws were about to expire. "What goes into a man's mouth does not make him 'unclean,' but what comes out of his mouth, that is what makes him 'unclean' " (Matthew 15:11). Within a generation, Jewish Christians considered the laws of Moses replaced by the prophesied "new covenant" (Jeremiah 31:31). Most Jewish groups still observe the food laws, with the exception of Reform Jews. They argue that without the temple—which the Romans destroyed—the laws "fail to impress the modern Jew with a spirit of priestly holiness."

◄ **A ROMAN PIG JOKE** "I would rather be Herod's pig than his son." That's what Caesar Augustus said about Herod the Great, according to one Roman writer. This was funny for two reasons. First, the Greek words looked and sounded similar: "pig" is *hys (HOOS)*, "son" is huios (HWEE os). Second, pigs were safer from the king. Herod executed three of his sons, fearing a coup. But as an observant Jew, he would have no reason to lay a hand on a pig.

FRESH MEAT FLOWN IN

A stubby common quail with a repeating name, the *Coturnix coturnix* is a quarter pounder about half the length of a foot-long dog. Though a weak flier, it manages to migrate from Europe to northern Africa and neighboring regions for the winter. Ancient Egyptian pictures show hunters netting quail in springtime grain fields. The Bible says wind drove a massive flock into the Hebrew camp, where the birds were eaten. There were apparently leftovers that weren't properly preserved, since the Hebrews soon got sick. The Bible calls it a plague—an apt description for food poisoning on a massive scale.

WHERE DID THE MANNA AND QUAIL COME FROM?

One month into their trek out of Egypt—sometime in May or June—Moses and the Hebrew refugees started running out of food.

Horrible timing. They were plodding across a rocky, barren stretch of the Sinai Peninsula that was called the Desert of Sin.

"If only we had died by the LORD's hand in Egypt!" the people complained to Moses. "You have brought us out into this desert to starve" (Exodus 16:3).

God quickly responded, and manna and quail rained from the sky.

Manna is Hebrew for "what is it?" The Hebrews had never seen anything like it. Manna covered the ground with thin flakes that looked like frost and tasted like honey. It arrived each morning—enough for two quarts per person. The exception was the Sabbath, when nothing came. But a double portion fell the morning before.

These mystery flakes—according to the most popular theory—were insect droppings. In May through June, parasitic insects bore sap from tamarisk trees, and excrete what they can't digest. The desert sun evaporates the liquid carbohydrate balls that are as large as peas. Flakes remain. Nomadic Arabs still call this manna, and use it as a sweetener.

The quail may have been the stubby, short-winged game bird that migrates to Europe from its winter home in Africa. Weak fliers, they lumber low and slow—the Bible spots their altitude at "three feet above the ground" (Numbers 11:31). Exhausted by their long-distance journey and fighting a wind that blew them off course, they were easy pickings.

◄ GATHERING MANNA Hebrews gathered manna flakes that fall overnight with the dew. Women grinded it into flour and make sweet-tasting flat cakes.

▲

BADLANDS OF SIN

The Desert of Sin doesn't look like a typical desert with rolling mounds of sand. It looks more like a strip-mining operation in rocky badlands. Barren mountains begin their jagged rise, and deep ravines scar the lowlands. Here is where manna began to fall.

◄ **MANNA FROM SAP** Older theories say manna was fungus-like lichen growing on rocks, or perhaps dried tree sap. A newer theory says manna came from insects secreting sap they couldn't digest, as pictured here. The Bible confirms that manna "looked like resin" (Numbers 11:7) before drying into white flakes. But insects produce these secretions just a few weeks each summer. Yet the Bible says God sent manna year-round—for forty years.

Mediterranean Sea

CANAAN

● Alexandria

● Rameses

GOSHEN

Desert of Sin

● Memphis

Nile R.

Gulf of Suez

▲ *Mt. Sinai*

A QUAIL IN THE ALPHABET
Yellow quail chicks have appeared in Egyptian hieroglyphic writing since about 5000 BC. The drawing stands for letters *W* and *U*—the sound of a long *O*, as in "shoot."

WATER IN THE ROCK Moses strikes a rock with his staff, and water pours out—enough for all the people and their livestock. Water can collect inside porous sedimentary rock. Savvy desert dwellers know that if they can see any slight seepage of water from a rock, they can break open the rock and often find enough water to drink, but not usually enough for thousands of people.

WHY DIDN'T GOD LET MOSES INTO THE PROMISED LAND?

Moses made just a tiny mistake. At least that's how the story reads in the Bible. Yet God banned him from ever setting foot in the Promised Land now called Israel.

It's hard to imagine a worse punishment for Moses, who led the Hebrew refugees for forty years with one goal in mind: get them to the Promised Land.

The question scholars have not been able to answer is why God wouldn't let Moses go with them. The Bible's story offers only slight clues.

Camped at an oasis in Kadesh, the Hebrews complained there was no water. God's instructions to Moses seemed simple enough: "You and Aaron must take the staff and assemble the entire community. As the people watch, command the rock over there to pour out its water" (Numbers 20:8 NLT).

Moses assembled the people. "Listen, you rebels!" he shouted. "Must we bring you water from this rock?" Then he struck the rock twice with the staff, and water gushed out.

God's response to Moses is a shocker: "Because you did not trust me enough to demonstrate my holiness to the people of Israel, you will not lead them into the land I am giving them!" (Numbers 20:12 NLT).

Four main theories attempt to justify God's harsh punishment:

1. God told Moses to simply "command the rock." But Moses struck it. Twice.

2. Moses claimed that the power came from him and Aaron: "Must we bring you water from this rock?"

3. Moses got angry and spoke "rash words" (Psalm 106:33).

4. The writer never mentioned the real sin because he wanted to treat Moses respectfully.

▲ **GLIMPSING THE PROMISED LAND** Standing on Mount Nebo, this is the view of the Promised Land Moses would have seen just before he died. The Bible says he could see the entire land, from the Jordan River west to the Mediterranean Sea, and from the Sea of Galilee in the north to the Negev Desert in the south. After witnessing what must have been a fulfilling sight, Moses died and was buried in an undisclosed location. The day of his death—which Jewish tradition says was the seventh of Adar (in February or March)—has become a Jewish memorial day for people whose gravesite is unknown.

▶ **WATER FROM ROCK FOR PHARAOH** Seti I reigned as Egypt's king from 1306 – 1290 BC—within about a century of Moses's lifetime. Seti did what some say Moses didn't do: give credit to a deity for water that came from a rock. Seti dug a well in the Eastern Desert mountains between the Nile River and the Red Sea. A temple dedicated to the king preserves his words of praise: "He [god] made water come out of the mountain for me."

▲ **BURNING BUSHES** The forty years Moses spent in God's service leading the Hebrews began at a burning bush near Mount Sinai. The bush may have been the *Dictamnus albus*, also known as the gas plant. It releases a vapor that can burn without harming the plant. Another contender: *Acacia seyal*. A volcanic vent could have ignited the bush, which turned to charcoal and kept burning for some time.

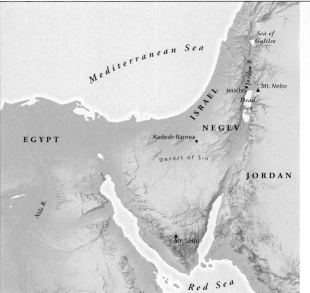

PUTTING SIN ON THE MAP

The sin of Moses—whatever it was—took place at the oasis of Kadesh Barnea, in a rugged wasteland on Egypt's side of the Egypt-Israeli border. The Hebrews spent most of their forty years in the wilderness at this oasis, which is watered by a huge spring. God allowed Moses to lead the Hebrews to Jordan's side of the Jordan River, but not into the Promised Land of Israel. Moses died at age 120 on Mount Nebo.

◄ **HEBREWS TAKE THE HIGH GROUND** Joshua's invasion of Canaan targeted mainly the hilly regions, according to battle reports from the Bible. This favored the Hebrews. It was easier for them to surprise the enemy. And Israel's vast, lightly-armed militia could swarm the hills and maneuver more easily than heavily-armed Canaanite soldiers and charioteers. After conquering the highland cities, Joshua divided the land among twelve tribes and assigned the tribes to mop up their individual regions.

WHY DID GOD ORDER ALL CANAANITES SLAUGHTERED?

One harsh word sums up the rules of engagement for Hebrew warriors fighting Canaanites, to take from them the land now called Israel.

Genocide.

"Do not leave alive anything that breathes," Moses told the people on the brink of invasion. "Completely destroy them ... as the LORD your God has commanded you" (Deuteronomy 20:16–17).

The Jewish race, perhaps most famous today for the Holocaust they endured during World War II, attempted a holocaust of their own. The difference was that God ordered the Canaanite killings.

He did this for two reasons, the Bible says.

1. As God had predicted to Abraham, father of the Jews, the wickedness in Canaan eventually "reached its full measure" (Genesis 15:16). As God once cleansed the sinful world by sending a flood, he now intended to cleanse Canaan with a flood of invaders.

2. Moses warned that if the Hebrews allowed even Canaanite children to live, they would grow up and return to their pagan roots. "They will teach you to follow all the detestable things they do in worshiping their gods, and you will sin against the LORD your God" (Deuteronomy 20:16–18).

As it turns out, this wasn't just a warning. It was a prophecy. And it came true. The Hebrews didn't finish the job. Instead, they learned to live with Canaanite neighbors, and even adopted many of their horrifying practices—including human sacrifice. Several hundred years later, God used Babylonian invaders to cleanse the land of sinful Jews.

NEW JERSEY OF THE MIDDLE EAST

Modern Israel is about the size of New Jersey—some 250 miles north to south, and 70 miles at its widest stretch. Israel's 6.5 million people are surrounded by four Arab nations and the deep blue sea.

Its territory today, along with the Palestinian regions of the West Bank and the Gaza Strip, is roughly the size of ancient Canaan. When the Hebrews invaded to take back their homeland after 430 years in Egypt, they also took land from nations that attacked them along the way, in what is now Jordan and Syria. They settled on both sides of the Jordan River.

Canaanite altar at Megiddo, where humans were sometimes sacrificed. ▶

◀ *Astarte, Caananite goddess of love and war.*

▶ **CANAANITE FROM JOSHUA'S DAY** Israel's Canaanite enemies were bronze-skinned and bearded, depicted on this broken piece of pottery. The fragment dates to about 1600—1200 BC, roughly the time Hebrews invaded the Canaanite homeland, now called Israel. Some scholars say this invasion took place in the 1400s BC, while others say the 1200s BC. In either case, Canaanites had been living there for at least 1500 years when Joshua and his militia arrived to lay claim to the land God promised Abraham's descendents.

▼ **RELIGION OF SEX AND VIOLENCE** A row of Canaanite silver idols from about the time of the Hebrew invasion stands on display in the Israel Museum at Jerusalem—silent witnesses of a pagan faith. Worship rites included sex with temple prostitutes, apparently intended to stimulate the rain god, Baal—rain was considered his semen. Children were burned alive as sacrifices on altars such as the one pictured above, at Megiddo in northern Israel. Canaanites became as depraved as the people of Sodom and Gomorrah, some scholars say, which is why God sentenced them to death.

DID THE WALLS OF JERICHO REALLY COME TUMBLIN' DOWN?

By the time Joshua arrived to fight the battle of Jericho, the city had been a ghost town for 150 years. That's what Jericho's first archaeologist said after digging in the ruins for several summers, beginning in 1907.

His name was Carl Watzinger, and his controversial conclusion set in motion an archaeological see-saw.

His opinion sank after Jericho's next archaeologist, John Garstang, climbed on board in the 1930s. He said Jericho and its double walls were destroyed and burned in about 1400 BC—the very time when many experts say Joshua arrived.

Next up was Jericho's third archaeologist, Kathleen Kenyon in the 1950s. She agreed with the first view: Jericho's walls tumbled long before Joshua got there.

Though Kenyon's opinion is the one that most archaeologists support today, not everyone agrees. Archaeologist Bryant Wood, in 1990, said Kenyon overlooked important evidence—pottery, magical charms, and carbon-dated burnt debris—from Joshua's time. He said she rejected the 1400s date because of what she didn't find: imported Cyprus pottery from that time found elsewhere in Israel. Wood said she dug in the poor part of town, where people wouldn't have bought expensive imports. Yet most archaeologists seem unconvinced.

Archaeologists still conduct limited digs at Jericho from time to time. An Italian-Palestinian team in 1997 uncovered part of Jericho's collapsed wall. As long as the digging continues, perhaps the see-saw will keep teetering.

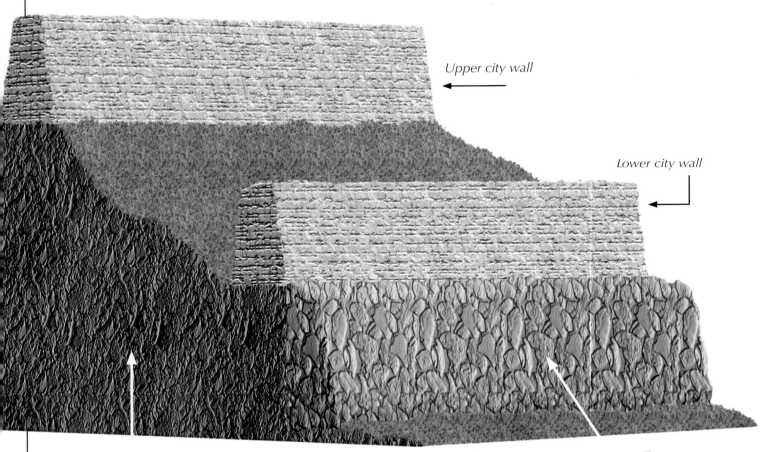

Upper city wall

Lower city wall

Earthen embankment

Retaining wall

▲ **TUMBLIN' DOWN** "At the sound of the trumpet, when the people gave a loud shout, the wall collapsed; so every man charged straight in, and they took the city" (Joshua 6:20). Because Jericho sits on a massive fault line, some speculate that an earthquake ripped down the city walls at the moment the trumpet sounded. Archaeologists confirm Jericho was surrounded by three walls. A stone retaining wall held the dirt mound in place. On top of that was a mud brick wall about six feet thick and perhaps a dozen feet high or higher. It collapsed outward, forming a ramp that invaders could use to climb up the retaining wall. Farther up the slope towered a second mud brick wall, with its base nearly fifty feet above ground level. The walls would have looked impregnable. Until they collapsed.

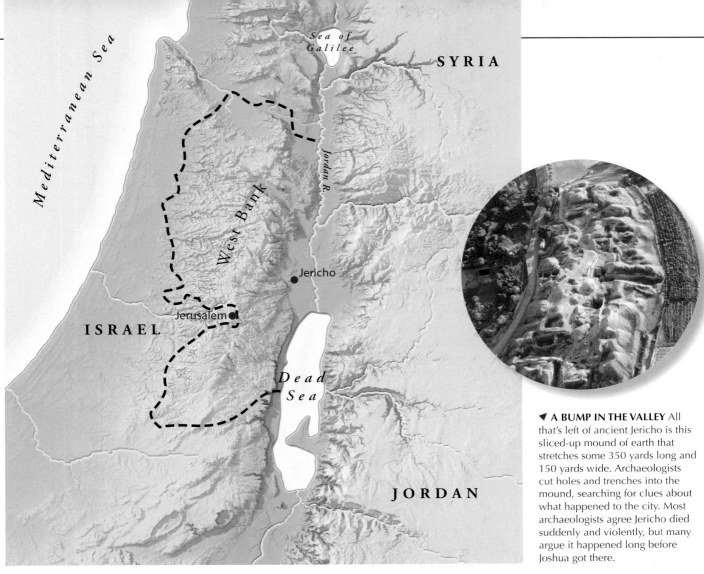

◄ A BUMP IN THE VALLEY All that's left of ancient Jericho is this sliced-up mound of earth that stretches some 350 yards long and 150 yards wide. Archaeologists cut holes and trenches into the mound, searching for clues about what happened to the city. Most archaeologists agree Jericho died suddenly and violently, but many argue it happened long before Joshua got there.

▲ ARAB JERICHO Fifteen miles east of downtown Jerusalem, Jericho is home to some 25,000 Palestinians. The city and its ten-acre mound of ancient ruins lie near the riverside border of the West Bank, a huge tract of land Israel captured from Jordan in a 1967 war.

JARS FULL OF GRAIN

Archaeologist John Garstang found many jars full of grain—one reason he believed this was the city Joshua destroyed. The Bible says Joshua's invasion took place after the spring harvest, that the siege was short—not long enough to starve the people out—and that God ordered the Hebrews to take nothing from Jericho. The pottery also seemed to match that of Joshua's day. Like cars today, pottery came in different styles during different times. Archaeologists assign dates to cities by the type of pottery they find.

DID THE SUN AND MOON STOP DURING JOSHUA'S BATTLE?

A coalition army of Canaanites surrounded the hill town of Gibeon, determined to wipe them out for signing a peace treaty with the invading Hebrews. So Gibeon leaders rushed a courier to Joshua with a frantic plea for help.

Joshua quickly assembled his militia and marched them all night up into the Judean hills. Then he surprised and routed the coalition forces with a morning attack.

It was during this battle that he prayed the most bizarre and baffling prayer in the Bible: "O sun, stand still over Gibeon, O moon, over the Valley of Aijalon" (Joshua 10:12). Apparently, the writer of Joshua's story quoted this prayer from the Book of Jashar, a collection of lost Hebrew poetry.

Some Christians take the story literally, arguing that the Creator could stop the earth from rotating, and still maintain gravity. In addition, some point out ancient but vague references to what might be a "long day," or to an urban legend about NASA discovering a lost day—which NASA not only denies, but says would be impossible for them to calculate.

Other Christians say Joshua's prayer was a poem that deserves poetic license. Perhaps Joshua was asking for strength to finish the battle. Or maybe he wanted relief from the intense summer sun—a prayer answered with cloud cover and a storm that produced hail. The Hebrew word Joshua used for "stand still" (*damam*) can also mean "stop shining." Yet the writer's report after Joshua's prayer suggests the sun stopped "and delayed going down" (Joshua 10:13).

▲ **KILLER HAIL** Hail the size of baseballs pummeled central Israel on October 16, 1992, in the same region where Joshua fought a Canaanite coalition that turned and ran for their lives. During the chase, "The LORD hurled large hailstones down on them [the Canaanites] … and more of them died from the hailstones than were killed by the swords of the Israelites" (Joshua 10:11).

SHAFTED

This water shaft discovered in the ruins of Gibeon adds credence to the Bible's story about how the people of Gibeon tricked Joshua into a peace treaty. Gibeon emissaries knew the Hebrews were supposed to kill all Canaanites, so they pretended to come from a distant country. Joshua agreed not to destroy the city, but to use the people as the Hebrews' "water carriers" (Joshua 9:21). Gibeon's water shaft—part of an elaborate water system—is cut thirty-seven feet wide and thirty-five feet deep through bedrock. The shaft stored water from a nearby spring, which people could reach through a tunnel, also cut from bedrock.

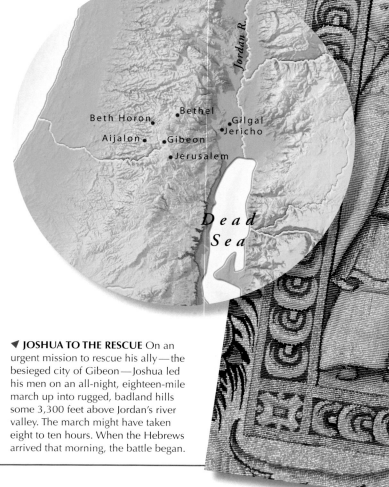

◀ **JOSHUA TO THE RESCUE** On an urgent mission to rescue his ally—the besieged city of Gibeon—Joshua led his men on an all-night, eighteen-mile march up into rugged, badland hills some 3,300 feet above Jordan's river valley. The march might have taken eight to ten hours. When the Hebrews arrived that morning, the battle began.

► **"SUN STAND STILL"** This was Joshua's mystifying prayer during a battle against five united Canaanite armies. Joshua also asked the moon to do the same. If he could see them both, it was probably around daybreak, with the sun rising in the east and the moon setting in the west.

▼ **SHADOWS IN REVERSE** Lying in bed seriously ill, King Hezekiah gets a sign from God that he will recover. The sun's shadow on a stairway moves backward ten steps. Unlike the story of Joshua, there appears to be no alternate way of reading this. The shadow moved backward, to the east. Some speculate a solar eclipse caused this. When the moon passes between the sun and earth, the moon's massive shadow zooms across the earth's surface at more than a thousand miles an hour—eastward. In addition to the massive shadow, there are small shadow bands that scientists say might be caused by refraction of light in the atmosphere.

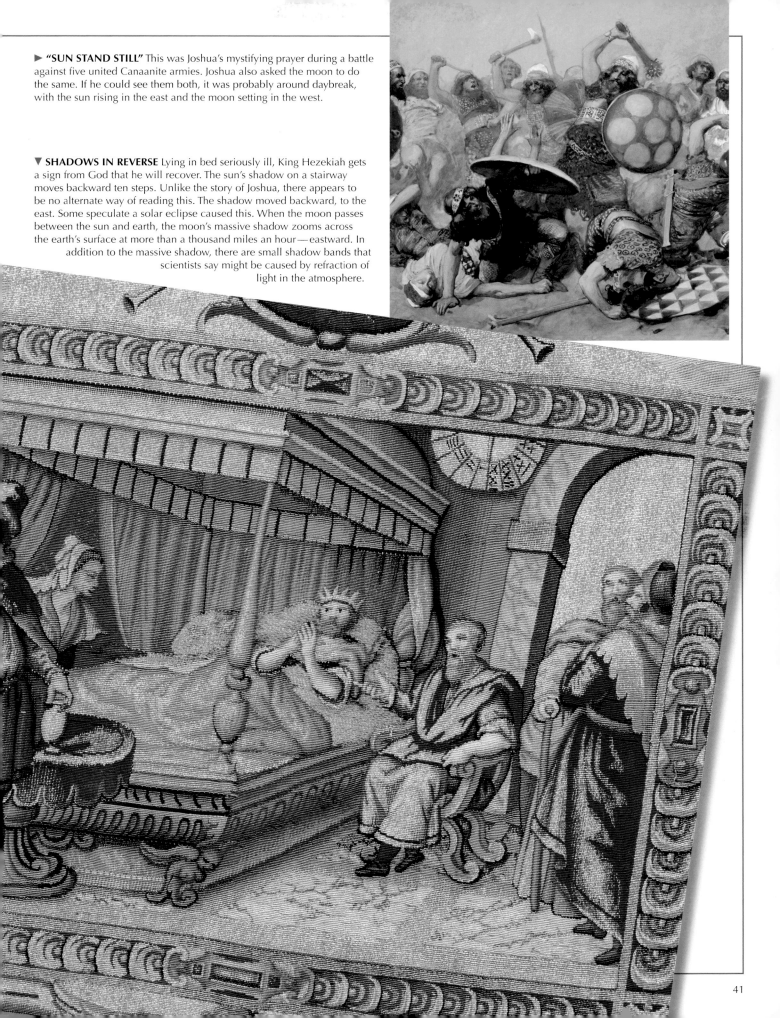

WHAT HAPPENED TO THE ARK OF THE COVENANT?

It seems strange the Bible never says what became of Israel's most sacred object, the ark of the covenant. It was the gold-covered chest that held the Ten Commandments and was kept in the Holy of Holies, the most sacred room in Jerusalem's temple.

Most scholars guess Babylonian invaders carried it off—or at least stripped the gold when they plundered and burned Jerusalem in 586 BC. Yet that raises the question of why Bible writers reported Babylonians stole the temple lampstands, bowls, and cups, but said nothing about the ark.

One legend preserved in Roman Catholic and Eastern Orthodox Bibles says that Jeremiah, the prophet who witnessed the fall of Jerusalem, hid the ark in what is now a Jordanian cave—on the mountain where Moses died (2 Maccabees 2:5).

There are other legends too.

Acting on one of them, a group of Knights Templar, who trace their heritage back a thousand years to the Crusades, have been using ground-penetrating radar to search for the ark and the Holy Grail (the cup Jesus used at the Last Supper) in ancient vaults beneath Rosslyn Chapel in Edinburgh, Scotland.

Christians in the Ethiopian Orthodox Church, however, insist the ark is in a small chapel at Aksum, Ethiopia, guarded by a lone monk and seen by no one but him. King Solomon sent it there, they say, so his alleged son with the Queen of Sheba—Menelik—could introduce the Jewish faith to people there.

Yet another possibility is that people are wearing the ark today. Its gold—which is the ultimate recycled metal—now rests in pieces on ringed fingers, pierced ears, and adorned necks.

◄ **SYNAGOGUE ARKS** Just as the Ten Commandments—the foundation for all Jewish laws—once rested in the ark of the covenant, Jewish Law today is written on scrolls and stored in synagogue enclosures called arks. This Law is known in Hebrew as the Torah, the first five books of the Bible. When it comes time to read from the Torah, a worship leader reverently takes the scroll from the ark.

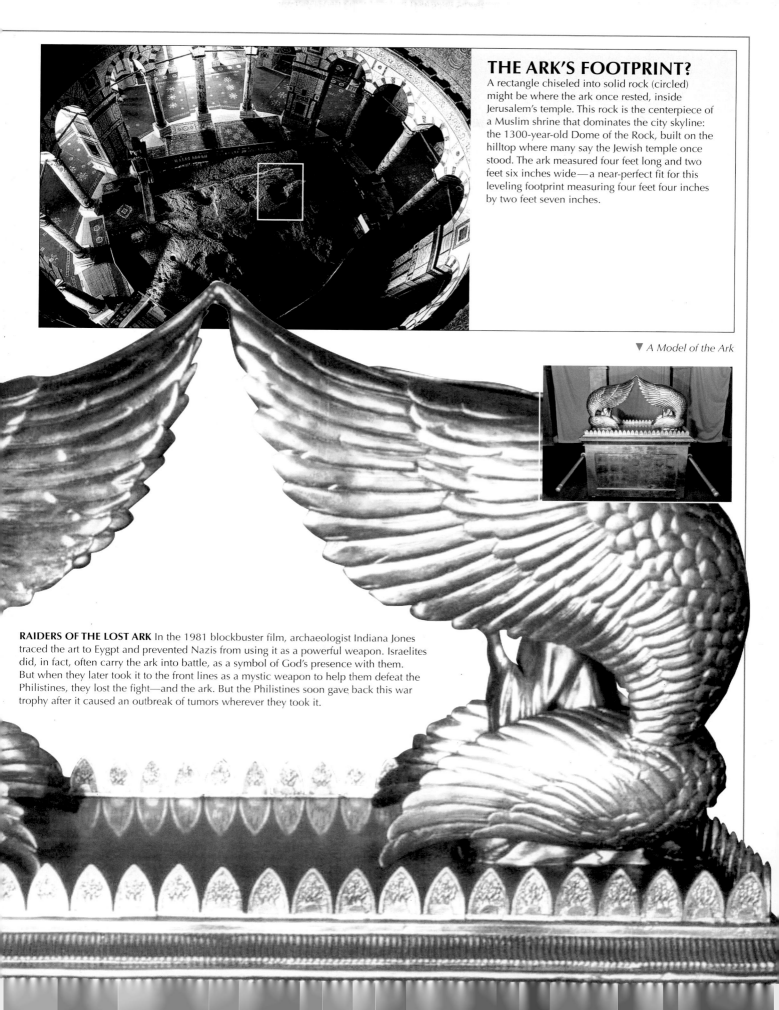

THE ARK'S FOOTPRINT?

A rectangle chiseled into solid rock (circled) might be where the ark once rested, inside Jerusalem's temple. This rock is the centerpiece of a Muslim shrine that dominates the city skyline: the 1300-year-old Dome of the Rock, built on the hilltop where many say the Jewish temple once stood. The ark measured four feet long and two feet six inches wide—a near-perfect fit for this leveling footprint measuring four feet four inches by two feet seven inches.

▼ *A Model of the Ark*

RAIDERS OF THE LOST ARK In the 1981 blockbuster film, archaeologist Indiana Jones traced the art to Eygpt and prevented Nazis from using it as a powerful weapon. Israelites did, in fact, often carry the ark into battle, as a symbol of God's presence with them. But when they later took it to the front lines as a mystic weapon to help them defeat the Philistines, they lost the fight—and the ark. But the Philistines soon gave back this war trophy after it caused an outbreak of tumors wherever they took it.

WHY DID A CHARIOT OF FIRE TAKE ELIJAH TO HEAVEN?

There's a short answer to the question of why the prophet Elijah was whisked away into the sky in "a chariot of fire" and "a whirlwind" (2 Kings 2:11).

No one knows for certain. The Bible doesn't say.

Yet there are clues in later Bible stories that might help explain Elijah's mysterious exit—clues that suggest his work on earth would not be finished until the messiah arrived.

The closing book of the Old Testament said God would send back "the prophet Elijah before the great and dreadful day of the Lord comes" (Malachi 4:5).

In time, Jews began thinking of Elijah as an advance man who would prepare the way for the messiah. Another prophet described the advance man as, "A voice of one calling: 'In the desert prepare the way for the LORD'" (Isaiah 40:3).

Jews developed many legends about Elijah, saying he sometimes returned to earth to help the poor and abused, and that he would one day come to bring peace to the world.

Jesus, however, said John the Baptist fulfilled prophecies about Elijah's return, "he is the Elijah who was to come" (Matthew 11:14). The angel Gabriel, too, said John would have "the spirit and power of Elijah" (Luke 1:17). John grew to become a prophet who introduced Jesus to the crowds. Yet Elijah's return wasn't just figurative. The Bible says he and Moses met with Jesus shortly before the crucifixion.

Perhaps Elijah's dramatic departure was intended to point the hopes of humanity to Jesus.

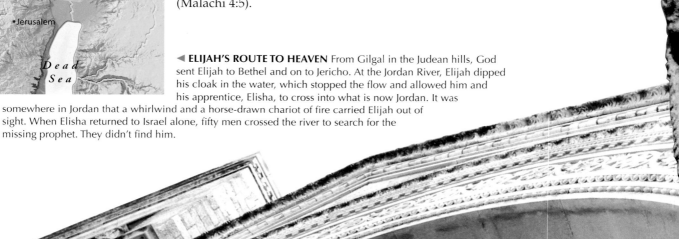

◄ **ELIJAH'S ROUTE TO HEAVEN** From Gilgal in the Judean hills, God sent Elijah to Bethel and on to Jericho. At the Jordan River, Elijah dipped his cloak in the water, which stopped the flow and allowed him and his apprentice, Elisha, to cross into what is now Jordan. It was somewhere in Jordan that a whirlwind and a horse-drawn chariot of fire carried Elijah out of sight. When Elisha returned to Israel alone, fifty men crossed the river to search for the missing prophet. They didn't find him.

ELIJAH'S RETURN ◄
The Church of the Transfiguration on Mount Tabor—six miles from Jesus' hometown in Nazareth—marks the place where tradition says Elijah made a reappearance to earth that was no less dramatic than his departure some 1200 years earlier. He and Moses appeared with Jesus on a mountain, shortly before Jesus headed to Jerusalem to be crucified. As Jesus stood with the two, his body was transfigured into what may have been a celestial, glowing form. Though Jesus refused the disciples' request to build a monument there, Christians built one in the fourth century AD—shortly after Rome legalized Christianity. Arab invaders destroyed the church, but Roman Catholic Franciscans built this church in the 1920s near the ancient ruins.

▲ **ELIJAH IN THE SKY** The Bible's story of Elijah's dramatic departure has, for centuries, captured the imagination of artists who painted the scene as they envisioned it. Some people today have a new take on what happened. They suspect Elijah got abducted by a UFO or sucked into a tornado. Yet the military image of a chariot fits the Bible's frequent teaching about spiritual warfare. A servant of Elijah's successor, Elisha, once panicked when a chariot corps surrounded their hometown. Elisha asked God to open the servant's eyes, and the man saw "the hills full of horses and chariots of fire all around Elisha" (2 Kings 6:17). Chariots of fire represented God's protection.

▶ **IS THIS CHAIR TAKEN?** When an eight-day-old boy is circumcised, the family leaves the door cracked open and a chair for the prophet Elijah. That's because Elijah is considered protector of the newborn. In addition, he might suddenly show up to announce that this child is the long-awaited messiah.

◀ **WARRIOR PROPHET** Aside from his flight to heaven in a fiery chariot, Elijah is perhaps most famous for executing Jezebel's 850 pagan priests and prophets. Elijah had challenged them to a battle of the gods, to see which deity—the Lord or Baal—could send fire from heaven to consume a sacrifice. Baal lost. This statue on Mount Carmel in northern Israel commemorates this battle for the faith of the nation.

▼ **A CUP FOR ELIJAH** Jews waiting for the messiah and his predecessor, Elijah, keep a cup of wine for the prophet at their annual Passover meal. Some say this is a way of expressing their hope that he will join them.

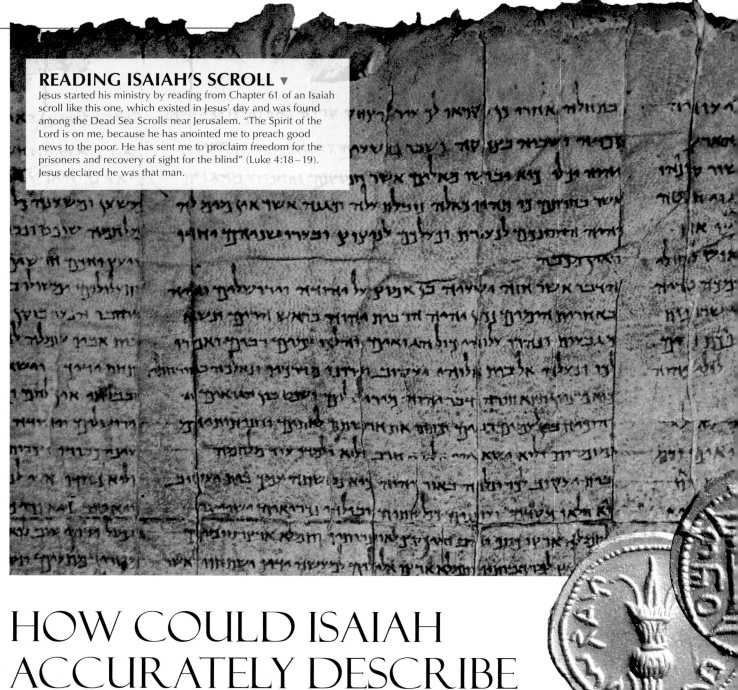

HOW COULD ISAIAH ACCURATELY DESCRIBE JESUS—700 YEARS BC?

To the Christian ear, many of Isaiah's words sound like an eye-witness report about Jesus—not prophecy from seven centuries before him.

"To us a child is born, to us a son is given.... And he will be called Wonderful Counselor, Mighty God, Everlasting Father, Prince of Peace" (Isaiah 9:6).

"He was pierced for our transgressions, he was crushed for our iniquities ... and by his wounds we are healed" (Isaiah 53:5).

Jewish scholars, however, insist Isaiah was talking about the Jewish nation, or some king, or perhaps a prophet—but certainly not Jesus. Many Christian scholars agree—at least partly. They say Isaiah probably had in mind the Jewish nation that would suffer in exile, but would later rise again. References to Jesus, some scholars explain, were overtones—signs pointing beyond the present, and extending far into the future.

If so, those overtones didn't slip past first-generation Christians who knew Jesus. New Testament writers quoted from Isaiah more than any other book, earning it the nickname of the Fifth Gospel.

How could Isaiah describe Jesus so accurately? If many Isaiah experts are right, it wasn't his intention at all. But New Testament writers show it was certainly God's intention.

▲ MESSIAH CONTENDERS
Various Jews throughout the centuries claimed they were the messiah who would usher in a new day of peace and prosperity. Most recently, many Jews made this claim of Rabbi Menachem Mendel Schneerson (1902–1994), charismatic leader of the ultra-conservative Lubavitch Jewish movement headquartered in Brooklyn. When the rabbi died, he wasn't replaced—some say because many followers expect him to return. A century after Jesus, many Jews endorsed another suspected messiah, Simon Bar Kokha. He led a doomed revolt against Rome in AD 132–135. His short-lived Jewish nation stamped their own coins with images of the temple the Romans had leveled fifty years earlier.

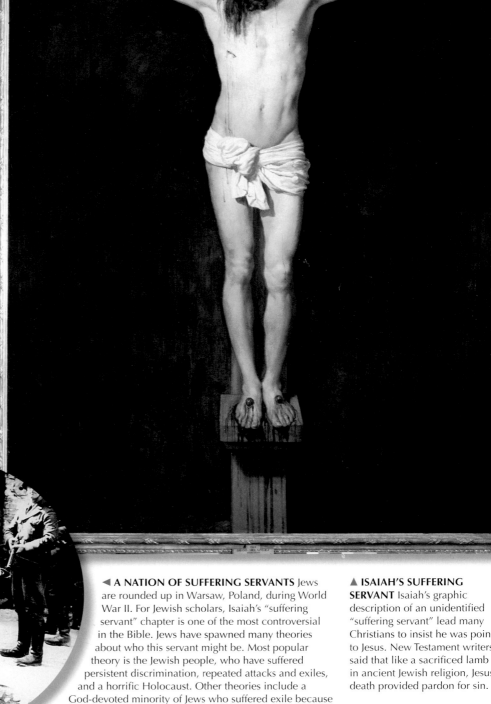

◄ A NATION OF SUFFERING SERVANTS Jews are rounded up in Warsaw, Poland, during World War II. For Jewish scholars, Isaiah's "suffering servant" chapter is one of the most controversial in the Bible. Jews have spawned many theories about who this servant might be. Most popular theory is the Jewish people, who have suffered persistent discrimination, repeated attacks and exiles, and a horrific Holocaust. Other theories include a God-devoted minority of Jews who suffered exile because of the nation's sins; Zerubbabel, who led the Jewish exiles home; the messiah, an ancient Jewish theory now unpopular.

▲ ISAIAH'S SUFFERING SERVANT Isaiah's graphic description of an unidentified "suffering servant" lead many Christians to insist he was pointing to Jesus. New Testament writers said that like a sacrificed lamb in ancient Jewish religion, Jesus' death provided pardon for sin.

DID A BIG FISH REALLY SWALLOW JONAH?

Though Bible experts have accepted Jonah's remarkable story for more than 2,000 years, in the last couple of centuries some have started questioning it—wondering if it's more parable than history.

Jonah son of Amittai was certainly a prophet. That's confirmed in 2 Kings 14:25, which says he lived in a small village in northern Israel during the 700s BC. But there's no mention of him or his mission to Nineveh in the vast, recovered records of that city. So some scholars wonder if an insightful writer, centuries later, took Jonah's name and made him the star of a short story that packs a powerful theological punch. On the other hand, Jesus spoke of Jonah in the belly of the fish. And that leads some Bible experts to conclude that Jesus considered the book of Jonah something more than a make-believe fish story.

God told Jonah to go to Nineveh, capital of the world's superpower, the vicious empire of Assyria. Jonah's mission: warn the people that their city would be destroyed.

Jonah tried to run away, boarding a ship but getting caught in a storm. Sailors threw him overboard to calm the storm, and a large fish swallowed him. Three days later the fish spit him onto a beach. Jonah delivered God's message, the people of Nineveh repented, God withdrew his punishment, and Jonah pouted under the shade of a vine because his single prophecy didn't come true. God killed the vine, which made Jonah even angrier.

God abruptly ends the story with a jarring thunderbolt of a statement—much as Jesus later ended his parables. God said if Jonah could show concern about a measly vine, God could show concern for more than 120,000 repentant people.

Parable or history, it's hard to miss the point that God cares about everyone—not just the Jews.

▲ **WAS IT A WHALE?** Some wonder if it was a sperm whale—like the one pictured here—that swallowed Jonah. They consume about a ton of food a day. Though they eat mostly fish, their favorite meal is deep-water giant squid—which can reach sixty feet long. The Bible describes the creature that swallowed Jonah only as "a great fish" (Jonah 1:17). Perhaps the Bible isn't more specific because Jonah—swallowed in a furious storm—never saw the creature. And since most Jews were sea-fearing shepherds and farmers, Jonah might not have recognized it even if he saw it.

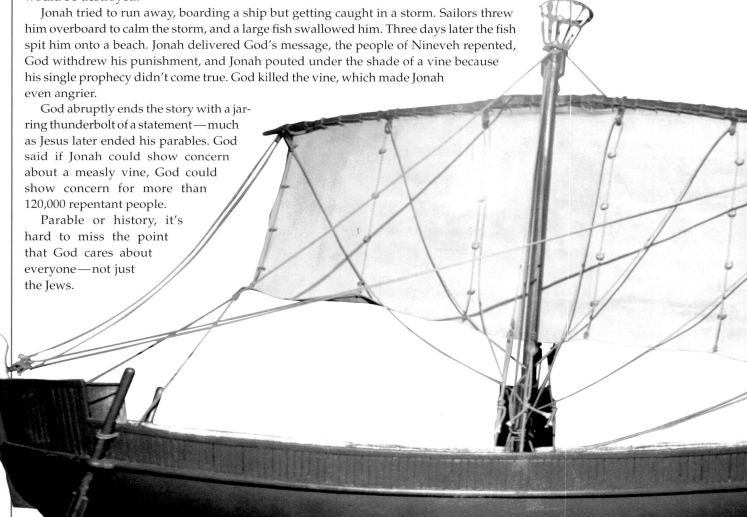

▼ **JONAH'S SEA CRUISE** A large sea creature returns Jonah to the shore after carrying him in its stomach for three days. Jesus spoke of this when predicting his own death and burial. "For as Jonah was three days and three nights in the belly of a huge fish, so the Son of Man will be three days and three nights in the heart of the earth" (Matthew 12:40). This is evidence, some experts say, that Jesus considered Jonah's story to be as historically accurate as the crucifixion and resurrection.

The Modern Jonah.

◄ **MODERN JONAH, AN URBAN LEGEND** The once prestigious New York World newspaper—owned by Joseph Pulitzer, whose will established journalism's Pulitzer Prizes—published this illustration on April 12, 1896. It's based on a story about a British sailor named James Bartley who survived a day and a half inside a sperm whale in 1891 before his shipmates harpooned the creature and cut Bartley free—alive but bleached white from gastric acid. Though Bartley was supposedly whaling off the Falkland Islands near Argentina on the *Star of the East*, his name isn't on the crew register. And the captain's wife later said the sailor was telling a whopper.

Black Sea

Caspian Sea

ASSYRIAN EMPIRE

Mosul (Modern) • • Nineveh

← Tarshish (Spain?)

Euphrates R.

Tigris R.

Mediterranean Sea

Baghdad (Modern) •

Gath Hepher •
Joppa •
• Jerusalem

JONAH'S U-TURN

God ordered Jonah east to Nineveh, capital of the feared Assyrian Empire near what is now Mosul, Iraq. Jonah was to warn them that because of their wickedness God was going to destroy the city. That would have been a bit like sending a Jew to Berlin with a similar message for Hitler in the early 1940s. Jonah headed west. He booked passage on a ship at Joppa bound for Tarshish, perhaps in Spain. A large fish intercepted Jonah during a storm and deposited him on the beach, pointing him back in the right direction.

DOES PRAYER CHANGE GOD'S MIND?

Though it may seem impossible to change the mind of someone who knows everything, the Bible tells several stories about God backing off of his plans to kill people. Each time, it was prayer that made the difference.

When the Hebrews of the Exodus started worshiping a golden calf, God vowed to "destroy them all" (Exodus 32:10). Moses convinced God not to.

When King Hezekiah got sick, God warned that Hezekiah wouldn't recover. Devastated, the king wept and prayed, "Remember, O Lord, how I have walked before you faithfully and with wholehearted devotion and have done what is good in your eyes" (Isaiah 38:3). God suddenly announced, through a prophet, that Hezekiah would live fifteen more years. What's intriguing about God's message is that he didn't seem motivated by Hezekiah's good works—which the desperate king seemed to use as a bartering tool. God said he was moved by the king's plea and tears.

It was also the repentant plea of Nineveh—Assyria's capital in modern-day Iraq—that convinced God to reverse his decision to destroy the city. Though Jonah was upset to come away looking like the prophet who cried wolf, God insisted he had a right to show mercy to the Assyrians.

If prayer doesn't change God's mind, theologians say, at least it changes people. So God's plans change because the people have changed.

▶ **PRAYER PHILOSOPHER** The Danish religious philosopher, Søren Kierkegaard, is shown here in a sketch by his cousin from around 1840. Kierkegaard, who remains a favorite source of insight for theologians today, once wrote, "Prayer does not change God, but changes him who prays."

◀ **PRAYER TOUR** A Roman Catholic priest leads a tour group through Jerusalem's Church of the Lord's Prayer. The walls are decorated with the Lord's Prayer written in sixty-two languages. When Jesus taught his disciples how to pray, he told them not to use prayer to impress people or manipulate God.

◄ JESUS ASKED BUT DIDN'T RECEIVE Hours before his crucifixion, Jesus prayed in the garden of Gethsemane: "My Father, if it is possible, may this cup be taken from me" (Matthew 26:39). Jesus didn't want to die. Even so, he ended his prayer in an attitude of submission: "Yet not as I will, but as you will." Theologians advise Christians to do the same. Though Jesus taught this about prayer: "If you believe, you will receive whatever you ask for" (Matthew 21:22), people who believe in God trust him enough to ask their question in a spirit of submission.

▼ AGAINST THE WALL An Orthodox Jew prays at the Western Wall, the world's most sacred site for Jews. This former retaining wall at the base of a Jerusalem hilltop is all that's left of the Jewish temple. Romans destroyed the temple in AD 70. A 1300-year-old Muslim shrine called the Dome of the Rock sits on the hilltop now. Since Solomon built the first temple, Jews have faced it when they prayed. Ancient Jewish writings also advise people to keep their prayers short, and to "know before whom you stand" (Berakhot 28b).

GOD'S QUICK RESPONSE

Gabriel arrives with a message for the prophet Daniel, who has been praying for the forgiveness of himself and his people. "As soon as you began to pray," Gabriel says, "an answer was given, which I have come to tell you, for you are highly esteemed" (Daniel 9:23). Centuries later, a New Testament writer says much the same thing: "The prayer of a righteous man is powerful and effective" (James 5:16).

WANDERING JEWS God made the Jews a promise: "I will take the Israelites out of the nations where they have gone. I will gather them from all around and bring them back into their own land. I will make them one nation in the land" (Ezekiel 37:21). Some Jews teach that as more and more of their people scattered around the world return to Israel, fulfilling prophecy, the messiah will soon join the reunion.

WHAT HAPPENED TO ISRAEL'S LOST TRIBES?

If legends from many different cultures are true—and genetic testing suggests that at least some of them are—Israel's tribes that have been lost for 2,700 years are now beginning to turn up in the strangest places.

When the Hebrews settled in what is now Israel, they divided the land among descendents of Jacob's twelve sons. Each tribe, named after a son, got its own territory. The nation split into two in 922 BC. The northern tribes appointed their own king, called themselves Israel, and made their capital in Shechem. The southern tribes covering the territory of Judah, Benjamin, and Simeon took the name of the largest tribe, Judah, and retained the capital of Jerusalem.

Two hundred years later, Assyrian invaders from what is now Iraq conquered the northern tribes, exiled most of them, and resettled the land with foreign pioneers. These tribes never returned, and many scholars say they were probably assimilated into other cultures. Most Jews today are thought to descend from the two southern tribes, which were conquered and exiled by Babylonians but were allowed to return home about half a century later.

Since at least the time of Christ, Jewish scholars insisted that the lost tribes still lived east of the Euphrates River that slices through Iraq. In fact, many communities east of the river—in Kurdish regions, Afghanistan, Pakistan, and India—claim a Jewish heritage. Recent DNA testing has confirmed Jewish links for some groups, including a community of people in India. They call themselves Bene Israel, "Sons of Israel."

52

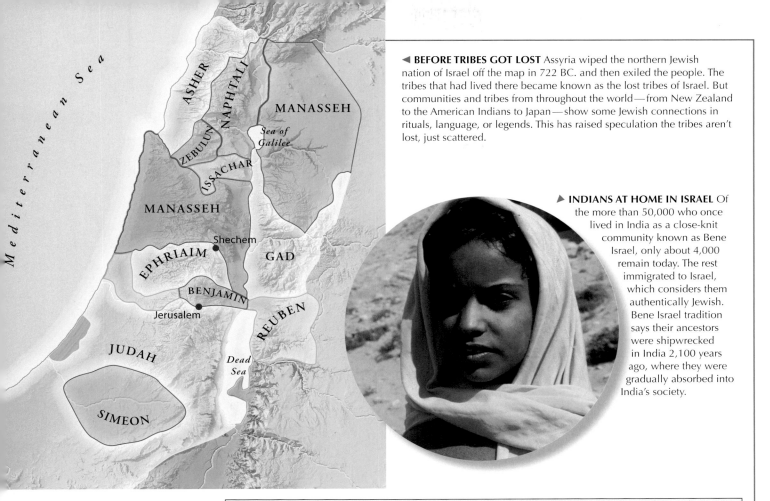

ASHER
NAPHTALI
ZEBULUN
ISSACHAR
MANASSEH
Sea of Galilee
MANASSEH
Shechem
EPHRIAIM
GAD
BENJAMIN
Jerusalem
REUBEN
JUDAH
Dead Sea
SIMEON

Mediterranean Sea

◄ **BEFORE TRIBES GOT LOST** Assyria wiped the northern Jewish nation of Israel off the map in 722 BC. and then exiled the people. The tribes that had lived there became known as the lost tribes of Israel. But communities and tribes from throughout the world—from New Zealand to the American Indians to Japan—show some Jewish connections in rituals, language, or legends. This has raised speculation the tribes aren't lost, just scattered.

► **INDIANS AT HOME IN ISRAEL** Of the more than 50,000 who once lived in India as a close-knit community known as Bene Israel, only about 4,000 remain today. The rest immigrated to Israel, which considers them authentically Jewish. Bene Israel tradition says their ancestors were shipwrecked in India 2,100 years ago, where they were gradually absorbed into India's society.

AFRICAN JEWS

Jews in Ethiopia, in northern Africa, worship in their synagogue. The Lemba tribe in southern Africa has a legend about a man named Buba leading them out of Israel long ago. Few believed them, even though they practice many Jewish customs, including circumcision, resting on the Sabbath, and not eating pork. The credibility of their legend got a big boost when recent genetic testing showed that they had Jewish DNA markers. One marker is the "Cohen genetic signature," common among Jewish men named Cohen (meaning "priest"), thought to have descended from Israel's first priest, Aaron. The percentage of Lemba tribesmen with this marker (9 percent) is about two to three times higher than in most Jewish groups (3 to 5 percent). For the founder's clan, the percentage soared to 53 percent.

▲ **NOT LOST YET** Writing a few years after Jesus in the first century AD, a Jewish historian named Josephus wrote in his book *Antiquities of the Jews* that "the ten tribes are beyond the Euphrates River even now, and there are so many of them that it's impossible to estimate the numbers."

WHAT WAS THE STAR OF BETHLEHEM?

After Jesus was born, sages known as Magi arrived in Jerusalem with an incredible story. They said they had come from the east—and followed a star. They said this star marked the birthplace of a baby who would become "king of the Jews" (Matthew 2:1).

Ancient writers tell similar stories, including one of a star guiding the Trojan prince Aeneas to the site where he founded the city of Rome.

Jews throughout the Middle East were expecting the messiah to arrive soon and free them from Rome. Suetonius, a Roman historian living in the first century, confirms that "throughout the entire East there had spread an old and persistent belief ... men coming from Judea would seize power."

It's unclear what "star" led the Magi to the Messiah.

Some suggest it was an exploding star—the supernova that Chinese and Korean astronomers said they saw during March and April in 5 BC. But Romans, who were also students of the sky, never reported it.

Others argue that since the Magi said the star moved, it may have been a celestial being that led the scholars, much like God once led the Hebrew exodus using a pillar of fire.

The most popular theory is that the star was a rare conjunction of planets that looked like a morning star. In the spring of 7 BC, Jupiter, which astronomers said represented kings, lined up with Saturn, which represented the Jews. This took place in the constellation Pisces, which represented Palestine—now Israel. Guided by this star map, the Magi knew exactly where to go: Jerusalem, capital of the Jewish homeland.

Gold

GREGORIVS · XIII · PONT · MAX

◄ **THE JESUS CALENDAR** Pope Gregory XIII, who served from 1572–1585, gave us the "Gregorian" Christian calendar we use today. Unfortunately, the pope drew from mistaken calculations. Jesus was not born on December 25, a week before January 1, AD 1. Roman records show that King Herod—who tried to kill the infant Jesus—died in 4 BC. To protect his family's right to rule, Herod ordered the execution of all Bethlehem boys ages two and under. That means Jesus was probably born sometime between 6 and 4 BC.

STRANGERS BEARING GIFTS

The wise men were "Magi," religious scholars who often advised royalty, and who searched for knowledge about the future by studying stars and religions. The Bible doesn't say there were three of them. That tradition developed apparently because of the three gifts they brought. About a thousand years after Jesus, names emerged for wise men: Gaspar, Melchior, and Balthasar. Embedded into the marble floor, a silver star marks the traditional place of Jesus' birth in Bethlehem's Church of the Nativity.

Frankincense

◀ **GIFTS FIT FOR A KING** Gold, frankincense, and myrrh are gifts the Magi brought—gifts worthy of royalty, as palace documents reveal. The gold could have come in any form, such as this Persian coin. The amber resin called frankincense comes from sap of various Boswellia trees in Saudi Arabia and Africa, and was burned as incense and used as perfume. So was myrrh, harvested as sap from Commiphora bushes. It's unknown what Joseph and Mary did with the gifts. Perhaps they sold them to pay for their trek to Egypt, to escape King Herod's execution of Bethlehem's baby boys.

Myrrh

▼ **TRACKING THE MAGI** Wise men who followed the star of Bethlehem came somewhere from the east—perhaps from Babylon in what is now Iraq or Susa in what is now Iran. We don't know how old Jesus was when they arrived. But King Herod ordered Bethlehem boys slaughtered up to age two "in accordance with the time he had learned from the Magi" (Matthew 2:16). Perhaps that's when the Magi first saw the star. It could have taken them several months to organize a caravan with an armed escort, and another two months or more to make a thousand-mile journey.

Euphrates R.

Tigris R.

Mediterranean Sea

Jerusalem
Bethlehem

Babylon

Susa

ARABIA

Persian Gulf

Red Sea

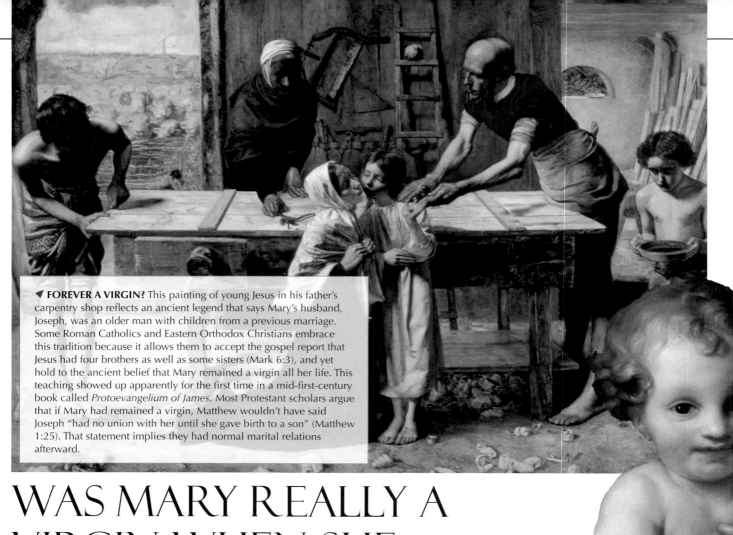

WAS MARY REALLY A VIRGIN WHEN SHE DELIVERED JESUS?

Even some Christians—in ancient times and today—have found it hard to believe that Mary conceived Jesus without having sexual relations.

Biology 101 says it's impossible.

Beyond biology, some argue that the virgin birth doesn't make sense for theological reasons. For one thing, they insist that it makes Jesus more than human—suggesting he didn't fully share in our humanity or serve as a model we can follow. And for another, they argue that it sends the message that sex is dirty—something God didn't want Jesus associated with.

Then there's the "virgin" translation problem. When Matthew said Jesus' miraculous birth fulfilled Isaiah's prophecy about a virgin giving birth to a son, the Hebrew word he quoted, *almah*, could refer to a young woman as well as a virgin. But the Greek word he uses (*parthenos*) almost always refers to a virgin. And the context clarifies Matthew's intention: "What is conceived in her is from the Holy Spirit" (Matthew 1:20). Luke, who used the same Greek word, reports Mary asking angel Gabriel how she could possibly become pregnant "since I am a virgin?" (Luke 1:34).

For reasons such as these, nearly every Christian group in early times embraced the virgin birth as a mysterious fact. When some fringe groups tried to teach otherwise, the majority effectively isolated them by inserting the virgin birth into formal statements of faith such as the Apostles' Creed, which is still repeated in many worship services.

▼ **WHAT CHILD IS THIS?** Jesus was the son of a Roman soldier, according to Celsus, the Egyptian philosopher who may have been Christianity's first scholarly critic. Writing in the AD 100s, Celsus said the soldier's name was Panthera, which was a common name. That's close enough to the Greek word for virgin, *parthenos*, that rabbis later speculated the gospel writers were using a subtle wordplay to reveal Jesus' true father.

TEEN MOTHER

The Bible doesn't say how old Mary was when she gave birth to Jesus. But if her father followed ancient Middle Eastern custom, he arranged for her marriage when she was about as old as this girl from the region today. Young women typically were engaged after their first monthly period started and married about a year later.

▶ **SON OF A GOD** In Greek stories, hero warrior Hercules was the son of a human woman and Zeus, ruler of all gods. Zeus tricked the woman by appearing in the form of her husband. In the birth of Jesus, however, there is no hint of sexual activity. A second-century theologian, Irenaeus, explained that just as God's Spirit created life at the beginning of time, the Spirit created new life in Mary—a fresh start for the human race.

▲ **CALL HIM JESUS** The angel Gabriel told Mary to name her son Jesus, meaning "the Lord is salvation." A common name at the time, Jesus is the Greek form of the Hebrew name Yeshua (Joshua)—inscribed here on a first-century stone burial box that held the bones of the dead.

WHY ARE SHADY WOMEN LISTED IN JESUS' FAMILY TREE?

Women don't usually show up in Bible genealogies. They weren't considered important enough.

Yet Matthew spotlights five dangling from the family tree of Jesus. That's surprising enough. But his choice of which five is a shocker.

He could have included revered women such as Sarah, Rebekah, Leah, Rachael, or Miriam. Instead, he chose

- Tamar, a widow whose father-in-law refused to give her another son to marry—so she disguised herself as a prostitute, seduced the elderly man, and had twins by him.
- Rahab, the Jericho prostitute who hid Hebrew spies.
- Ruth, a widow who bathed, splashed on perfume, and sneaked under the covers of a man she wanted to marry.
- Bathsheba, who committed adultery with King David.
- Mary, who got pregnant with Jesus out of wedlock.

It's understandable why Mary's on the list. But why the other women? Matthew didn't explain why, so we're left guessing.

One guess among many is that all of them except Jesus' mother was a non-Jew. So Matthew wanted to show that Gentiles played an important role in Jewish history, and that Jesus' message of salvation was for them, too.

Another guess is that all the women before Mary were involved in sex sins, but those women had since become accepted by Jewish leaders as respectable. Matthew may have included them to silence Mary's critics.

Yet another popular theory is Matthew was showing how God accomplishes his plans by working through unlikely people.

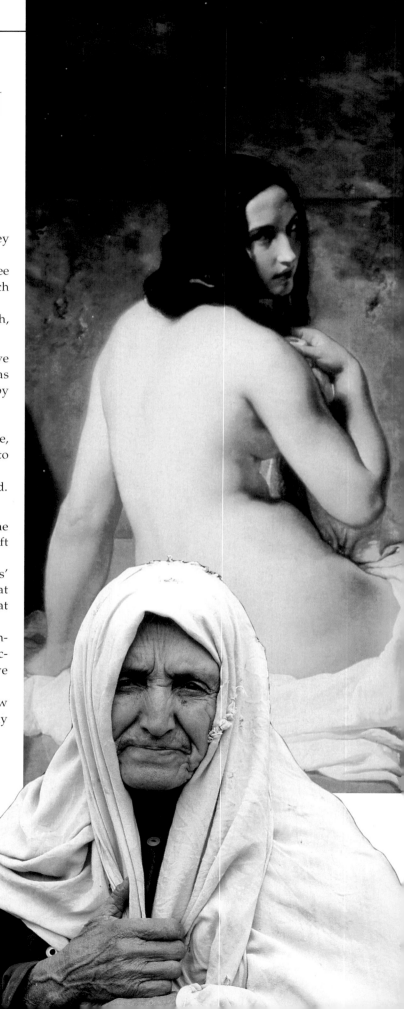

▶ **A WIDOW'S HARD LIFE** This widow, living in a cave outside Bethlehem, put on her best scarf for the photo. As part of the ancient system of welfare, a dead man's closest male relative was supposed to marry the widow. When the widow Ruth slipped under the covers with Boaz, a Bethlehem farmer related to her late husband, she was asking him to fulfill this obligation. Their son became King David's grandfather.

◀ BATHSHEBA IN HOT WATER

Bathsheba was a soldier's wife when King David saw her taking a bath and called her to his palace. It's unknown if she willingly engaged in the affair that led to her pregnancy and to David's murder of her husband. But one theory about why she's included in Jesus' family tree is that she and the other four women represent poor and powerless people Jesus came to serve. Throughout the rest of Matthew's gospel, Jesus criticizes the rich and powerful for abusing the weak.

▼ A HUMANITARIAN PROSTITUTE

The Rahab mentioned in Jesus' family tree was almost certainly the prostitute who helped the Hebrew spies that Joshua sent to Jericho. But she was later honored by Jewish scholars as well as a New Testament writer for obeying the commandment to feed and shelter the needy (Hebrews 11:31).

FOUR TERRIBLE SINNERS

One of the first known explanations about why Matthew chose the women he did for Jesus' family tree comes from Jerome. He was a scholar who in the AD 300s moved to Bethlehem to translate the Bible into Latin. He speculated that the four women besides Mary were chosen because of their terrible sins—to show that Jesus came to save even the worst sinners.

◀ HERE COMES THE BRIDE A

Bedouin woman prepares for her wedding ceremony. Four of the women in Jesus' family tree may have been non-Jewish brides: Tamar, probably a Canaanite; Rahab, a Jericho Canaanite; Ruth from Jordan, and Bathsheba married to a Hittite from what is now Turkey or Syria.

WHY DIDN'T JESUS WANT TO TURN WATER INTO WINE AT CANA?

Jesus and his mother, Mary, had a puzzling conversation at a wedding.

Mary told him the wine was gone. Though she didn't blame him, some scholars speculate that the wedding planners hadn't figured on Jesus bringing his dozen disciples.

"Dear woman, why do you involve me?" Jesus answered. "My time has not yet come" (John 2:4).

Though that sounds like a refusal wrapped in rebuke, Mary told the banquet servants to do whatever Jesus said. Surprisingly, Jesus turned six stone jars of water into wine.

Some scholars—in ancient times as well as today—say translators got Jesus all wrong. He agreed to Mary's request in a reply that sounded more like, "Why are you telling me what I can see for myself? The time of my suffering—when I won't be able to do miracles—isn't here yet." Other scholars say it's grammatically possible that Jesus' second sentence can be phrased as a question, "Hasn't my time come?" which implies he would help.

Either of these explanations might account for Mary's response of telling the servants to do whatever Jesus said, and Jesus performing the miracle.

But many scholars say the translators got it right. Jesus hesitated, perhaps because he knew that this—his first miracle—would set in motion an unstoppable chain of events leading to the cross. If so, shortly after Mary's request, Jesus received the assurance that his time had come.

▲ **CANA OF GALILEE** The small Galilean village of Cana was probably half a day's walk from Jesus' hometown of Nazareth, in what is now northern Israel. Located about eight miles northeast of Nazareth, a ruin called Khirbet Qana is currently the top contender for Cana. Though it's still unexcavated, scholars favor it partly because Cana means "reed" and the ruin lies in a marshy valley where reeds grow.

◄ **A JUG OF COLD WATER** The water Jesus turned into wine was stored in six stone jars like this—each jar containing twenty to thirty gallons. Only the gospel of John reports this miracle. Many Bible experts wonder if John—a master of metaphor—chose this as the first of seven miracles because of wine's symbolic connection to the coming messiah. Prophets had said that on the day of salvation, when God's kingdom came, there would be feasting and plenty of fine wine.

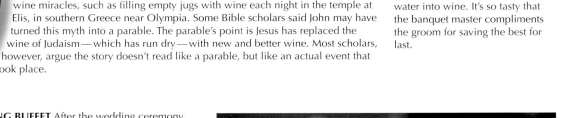

◀ **BORROWED MIRACLE?** Greek god of wine Dionysus, also called Bacchus, holds a horn filled with wine. Greek myths said this son of Zeus performed wine miracles, such as filling empty jugs with wine each night in the temple at Elis, in southern Greece near Olympia. Some Bible scholars said John may have turned this myth into a parable. The parable's point is Jesus has replaced the wine of Judaism—which has run dry—with new and better wine. Most scholars, however, argue the story doesn't read like a parable, but like an actual event that took place.

▲ **THE LAST SHALL BE BEST** In his first reported miracle, Jesus turns water into wine. It's so tasty that the banquet master compliments the groom for saving the best for last.

▼ **WEDDING BUFFET** After the wedding ceremony, guests are greeted with a buffet-diner's delight. Middle Eastern cuisine at this wedding banquet includes croissants, dough-wrapped meat hors d'oeuvres, stuffed grape leaves, and mini-pizzas. In Jesus' time, guests enjoyed not just one meal, but seven days of meals. That helps explain why the wedding planners underestimated how much wine they would need.

WEDDING BLESSING OVER WINE

A wedding guest raises a cup of wine while the Jewish couple receives their blessing, which occurs about halfway through the ceremony. Afterward, the couple and their guests seal this blessing with a sip of wine. In Bible times, wine was typically the groom's responsibility at the celebration. Running out of this staple drink was not only a social blunder—it was sometimes the source of lawsuits. By custom, people traveling a long way for the wedding expected an adequate supply of food and wine.

IS THE DEVIL A LIVING BEING, OR A SYMBOL OF EVIL?

In the beginning, there was no Satan—just a mysterious, unnamed "adversary."

In fact, *satan* is the Hebrew word for "adversary." So the Old Testament describes anyone opposing someone as a satan—including God and angels. An angel once told prophet Balaam, "I have come here to oppose [*satan*] you" (Numbers 22:32).

That doesn't mean there's no such creature as the devil.

But the Old Testament reveals almost nothing about him. The New Testament, however, says plenty. There we discover, for the first time, that he was the ancient serpent who tempted Eve.

Sometimes called the devil—from the Greek word *diabolos* for *satan*—he walked and talked with Jesus, trying to lure him away from God's plan of salvation. The Apostle Paul saw Satan as a personal being. Paul advised Christians, "Take your stand against the devil's schemes. For our struggle is not against flesh and blood, but against ... the spiritual forces of evil" (Ephesians 6:11–12).

In a shocking revelation, one writer declared "the whole world is under the control of the evil one." But that writer also added a note of assurance: "The one who is in you is greater than the one who is in the world" (1 John 5:19; 4:4).

SATAN WAS HERE

Faces as cold as barbed wire, an adult and child huddle together at Auschwitz, a World War II concentration camp where more than 1.5 million people were killed through gassing, starvation, and torture. Though most evangelical Bible experts portray Satan as an individual, some experts argue otherwise. They suggest he's a way of symbolizing evil at its worst—such as the depth of evil that tries to annihilate an entire race.

◄ **EXORCISM** A priest holds a crucifix to the mouth of a possessed girl in this scene recreating an exorcism. Ancient Jewish writings suggest that the success of an exorcism depended on both the personal force of the healer as well as what the healer said and did. Jesus once cast a demon out of a boy after his disciples had failed. When the disciples asked why they failed, Jesus explained, "Because you have so little faith" (Matthew 17:18).

▲ **"NO DEVIL, NO GOD"** That's how Methodist founder John Wesley, in the late 1700s, expressed his belief in a personal Satan. Wesley and many other Christian leaders have asked what people are saved from if not Satan and the evil he epitomizes and directs.

BOTTLED DEMON ▲

Off the southern coast of India lies the West Virginia-size island of Sri Lanka. There, a *kattadiya*—demon expert—holds a bottle said to contain an evil demon exorcized from a person. The *kattadiya*'s plan is to throw the bottle into the Indian Ocean. Jesus once transferred demons from a man into a herd of pigs, "and the whole herd rushed down the steep bank into the lake and died in the water" (Matthew 8:30). Some Bible experts say Jesus did this to prove the man was cured, but others suggest this transfer was somehow part of the cure.

◄ **PACT WITH A DEMON** This is a contract that a demon named Asmodee is said to have written for French priest and exorcist John Baptiste Gault. It translates to read, "I promise, in leaving the body of this creature, to make, below her heart, a slit the length of a pin [that will penetrate] at the same time her chemise [undergarment], bodice [corset] and dress. The slit will be bleeding. This will be tomorrow, the twentieth of May, at five o'clock in the afternoon, Saturday. I promise also that Gresil and Amand [two demons] will also make their openings, in a similar way, though smaller. And I ratify that which Leviatam, Behemot and Beherie [perhaps other demons] have promised to do [with] their companion, as a sign of their leaving, on this register made in the church of Saint Croix, on 19 May 1629. Asmodee."

WHY DOES GOD LET BAD THINGS HAPPEN?

One of the main reasons many people don't believe in God is because they see so much evil in the world.

They can't believe a good God would stand for it.

Christian thinkers have tried to explain evil. Sometimes, they say, God's behind it—or behind what at first glance appears evil. When disciples asked Jesus why a man had been born blind, Jesus answered, "This happened so that the work of God might be displayed in his life" (John 9:1). Then Jesus healed him.

Some evil comes from the freedom God gave people to choose. Without this freedom, scholars argue, we'd be fleshy robots incapable of love, mercy, or kindness—all of which are available only through freedom of choice.

Some evil comes from natural disasters, such as fire, earthquakes, or epidemics. Scholars say these weren't part of God's original creation, but that the sin of Adam and Eve changed creation—unleashing tragedy and death, "Cursed is the ground because of you ... dust you are and to dust you will return" (Genesis 3: 17–19). Original sin also changed humanity, many scholars say, corrupting the spirit and making people inclined to do harmful things to themselves and others.

Yet there's good news in suffering, some say. The good news is that suffering is a reminder that evil has already been defeated—as surely as the suffering Jesus rose from the grave.

In the end, most Bible experts admit there's no way to make sense of suffering. So they trust in the one who suffered for them.

◄ **LOOKING FOR A GOOD GOD** Pierre Bayle, French philosopher in the 1600s, argued that if God were completely good, he would destroy evil. Since he didn't, there was no such God.

► **THE DOWNSIDE OF FREEDOM** Augustine, a Christian theologian from the fifth century, said we shouldn't blame God when bad things happen—even though it was God who gave people freedom to choose evil. Augustine said freedom of choice is so important that God preferred to "bring good out of evil than to prevent the evil from coming into existence."

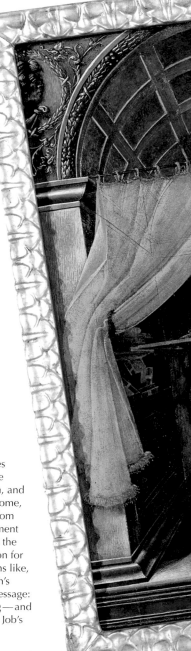

◄ **JOB'S TOTAL LOSS** Though Job does nothing to deserve it, his vast herds are stolen, his children die in a windstorm, and boils erupt all over his body. Friends come, bringing with them conventional wisdom of the day, that this was God's punishment for Job's secret sin. God himself enters the debate. Instead of explaining the reason for Job's suffering, he simply asks questions like, "Where were you when I laid the earth's foundation?" (Job 38:4). Job got the message: there's a limit to human understanding—and that's where faith begins. God restores Job's herds and gives him more children.

▲ **MOUNT VESUVIUS VICTIM** Remains of a child lie covered in volcanic ash after Mount Vesuvius erupted in AD 79—wiping out the Italian resort city of Pompeii, home to about 20,000. Some Christian thinkers in ancient times speculated that evil forces, such as demons, cause natural disasters like this. Many today argue that when the first humans sinned, it changed God's good creation—bringing a curse on the land. Others say people invite disaster by setting up residence in areas prone to such powerful forces of nature.

A SLAVE BECOMES SAVIOR

Fearing for their lives, Joseph's brothers ask forgiveness for selling him to slave traders when he was a teenager. Now pharaoh's highest official, Joseph shocks them with his reply, "You intended to harm me, but God intended it for good to accomplish what is now being done, the saving of many lives" (Genesis 50:20). Joseph invited his entire extended family to Egypt and saved them from starvation during a seven-year drought.

O BOTTICELLI (FILIPEPI)
ENTINO N.1444/45-M.1510
S. AGOSTINO

◀ **EGYPTIAN HERETIC** Arius (died 336), a minister in Alexandria, Egypt, taught that Jesus was divine but not God's equal. Like many scholars of his day, Arius thought Proverbs 8 was about God creating Jesus, "as the first of his works … before the world began" (8:22–23). So he reasoned that Jesus was less than God and subject to him—and that the Holy Spirit was subject to Jesus.

HOW CAN THERE BE THREE GODS IN ONE?

Most Jews don't believe Jesus is God.

With good reason, they argue. The Bible says, "Hear, O Israel: The LORD our God, the LORD is one" (Deuteronomy 6:4).

Not two. Or three.

In fact, the Bible never uses the word *Trinity.* The closest it comes is when Jesus tells his disciples to baptize people "in the name of the Father and of the Son and of the Holy Spirit" (Matthew 28:19).

Jesus knew what the Jews believed about God, yet he offered only a mystifying response, "I and the Father are one" (John 10:30).

Perhaps he knew the Trinity was an idea that physics-bound humans couldn't hope to understand. Yet many Jews and Gentiles alike believed he was God because he backed up his words with miracles that only God could do—calming storms, healing the sick, and raising the dead.

INTO THE JORDAN ▶
Christians visiting Israel today often follow the footsteps of Jesus into the Jordan River, where they are baptized just as he was. This ritual generally includes a reference to the Trinity that comes from Jesus' commission to his disciples: "Go and make disciples of all nations, baptizing them in the name of the Father and of the Son and of the Holy Spirit" (Matthew 28:19).

▼ MIRACLES INSTEAD OF AN EXPLANATION The Apostle John has long been considered the man who wrote the gospel of John. This unique gospel has one purpose above all, "That you may believe that Jesus is the Christ, the Son of God" (John 20:30). Oddly, John doesn't try to explain why Jews should believe this when they've always been taught there's only one God. Instead, he simply reports the divinity of Jesus as fact. Then he spends the rest of the book trying to prove it by presenting miraculous signs as the evidence—from the creation-style miracle of turning water into wine, to the next world-style miracle of raising Lazarus from the dead.

▲ MAJORITY OPINION Augustine (354–430) was a scholar in what is now Tunisia, on Africa's north coast. After centuries of debate, church leaders decided to accept by faith what they couldn't explain about the Trinity. Augustine summed up the consensus, "The Father is God, the Son is God, the Holy Spirit is God … yet we do not say that there are three gods, but one God, the most exalted Trinity."

THREE FOR THE BAPTISM
God the Father watches as the Holy Spirit descends like a dove at the baptism of Jesus, in this painting by Ottavio Vannini (1585–1643). The artist drew from a word picture in the Bible: "As Jesus was coming up out of the water, he saw heaven being torn open and the Spirit descending on him like a dove. And a voice came from heaven: 'You are my Son, whom I love; with you I am well pleased'" (Mark 1:10–11).

▲ **SCHOLARS AS CRITICS** Jewish elders study Scripture. Although many Jews embraced Jesus, religious scholars in Jerusalem were among Jesus' harshest critics. They so opposed his ministry that they attributed his most astonishing miracles to the power of Satan instead of God. This, Jesus said, was unforgivable.

◄ **SPIRIT BEING** The Holy Spirit descends on the disciples. Unlike God the Father and the Son, the Holy Spirit is never portrayed in the Bible as taking human form. Instead, he is often portrayed in art as a dove. That's because the New Testament says at the baptism of Jesus the Spirit descended like a dove.

WHAT IS THE UNFORGIVABLE SIN?

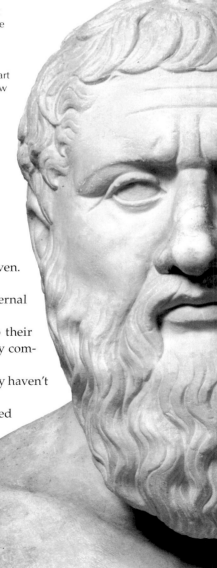

In a fit of anger, some people have told the entire godhead where to go—and it wasn't heaven. Then they came across these words of Jesus:

"Whoever blasphemes against the Holy Spirit will never be forgiven; he is guilty of an eternal sin" (Mark 3:29).

One of the most common reasons Christians throughout the centuries have gone to their minister for counseling is to talk about the unpardonable sin—because they thought they committed it.

Savvy ministers calm their people with the assurance that if they're worried about it, they haven't committed it.

Jesus was addressing Jewish scholars who had grown so narrow-minded and hard-hearted that they were incapable of recognizing their sin any longer—let alone repenting.

Jesus said they could be forgiven for attacking him, perhaps because Jesus understood how people could doubt him. But there was no excuse for failing to see God behind all the teachings and miracles of Jesus. Who but God could instantly heal so many sick people, control the forces of nature, and raise the dead?

"Satan," the Jewish scholars answered.

They were so spiritually blind that they looked God in the eyes and called him the devil. They were beyond hope.

◄ **LIE OF THE SOUL** Greek philosopher Plato may have captured the essence of what Jesus meant by blaspheming the Holy Spirit. In his book *The Republic,* written more than 300 years before Jesus, Plato spoke about the lie of the soul. He explained that "no one wants to lie to the most important part of himself.... to have lied to the soul about something real and true ... and to store the lie there."

▲ **DROP-DEAD DISOBEDIENCE** Ananias and his wife Sapphira (who arrives later), die instantly after giving a donation to the disciples. Both lied, saying they donated all the money from the sale of some land. Actually, they kept part of the money. Peter said they "lied to the Holy Spirit" (Acts 5:3). Some Bible experts point to this as an example of the unforgivable sin. Ananias and Sapphira denied the miraculous work the Spirit was doing among the church, and sought credit for themselves. Others, however, argue that though Ananias and Sapphira lost their lives, we can't presume they lost their salvation as well.

BE PERFECT

In his most famous sermon—the Sermon on the Mount—Jesus tells his eager listeners "Be perfect ... as your heavenly Father is perfect" (Matthew 5:48). Because it's impossible for humans to be as morally perfect as God, who's the author of perfection, many Bible experts say Jesus was raising the bar—calling believers to a higher life. The Aramaic word Jesus used can mean "whole" or "complete," as in fully devoted to God.

KISS OF DEATH When Judas greeted Jesus in the garden of Gethsemane, it wasn't with the endearing title of *Lord* the other disciples often used. It was with *Rabbi*, merely a teacher.

WHY DID JUDAS BETRAY JESUS?

▲ **DEATH SENTENCE** The *Temple Scroll* is one of the famous scrolls found in caves beside the Dead Sea. Dating to the time of Jesus, this scroll reveals a custom that might explain why Judas felt compelled to hang himself. "If there is a spy against his people who betrays his people to a foreign nation or causes evil against his people, you are to hang him from a tree so he will die."

By the time Jesus and his disciples gathered for the Last Supper on the night of his arrest, "the devil had already prompted Judas Iscariot, son of Simon, to betray Jesus" (John 13:2).

But it wasn't as simple as "the devil made me do it."

Satan, as portrayed in the Bible, is skilled at exploiting a person's natural desire, once tempting a fasting Jesus to turn stones into bread. Yet whatever Satan's involvement, Judas was responsible. "Woe to that man who betrays the Son of Man!" Jesus said. "It would be better for him if he had not been born" (Mark 14:21).

What desire did Satan exploit?

The most popular theory is that Judas joined the disciples because he thought Jesus was the kind of messiah Jews desperately wanted—someone who would drive out the Romans. As the theory goes, Judas thought the betrayal would force Jesus' hand. When he realized it didn't work and that Jesus was about to die, Judas killed himself.

Another theory says Judas wanted the reward. It's an idea that makes some sense in light of John's gospel, which identifies Judas as the group's treasurer who stole some of the money. Or perhaps his motive was to punish Jesus for failing to use his miraculous power to lead Israel to independence.

Whatever Judas' reason, he soon realized it didn't justify what was about to happen to Jesus. Overcome with remorse, Judas hung himself from a tree.

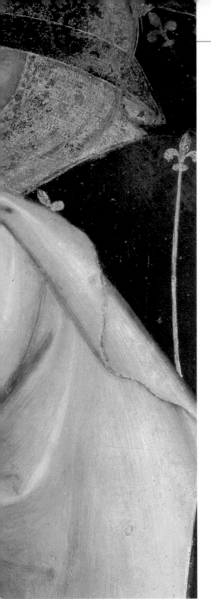

BLOOD MONEY ◄

A handful of silver drachmas. Temple officials paid Judas thirty coins for Jesus. The Bible doesn't say what type of coins, but one ancient manuscript describes them as staters—the most common coin Jews used to pay their temple tax. If this was Judas' reward, it was equal to about four months salary for a typical laborer. Though it's possible that money was one reason Judas turned Jesus in—since Judas asked temple officials what they'd pay—it probably wasn't the main reason. Judas didn't negotiate, and he later returned it.

SATAN AT THE LAST SUPPER Two gospels—Luke and John—report Satan entering Judas during the Last Supper. Jesus predicted the betrayal. He said the betrayer would be the person to whom he gave bread—then Jesus dipped a piece of bread into a dish and gave the bread to Judas. "As soon as Judas took the bread, Satan entered into him" (John 13:27). Judas left to help Jewish authorities arrest Jesus quietly without provoking a riot.

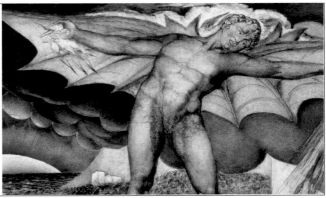

◄ **GARDEN BETRAYAL**
A small plug of ground with a few gnarled olive trees is all that remains of the olive grove on the Mount of Olives. Judas knew Jesus planned to pray in the garden of Gethsemane after supper, so he led the Jewish temple police there to arrest him.

WHY DID JESUS HAVE TO DIE?

Jews, Romans, and Christians all have different explanations for why Jesus had to die.

Jews said he died for blasphemy—claiming to be God's Son.

Romans said it was for subversion—claiming to be king when Caesar was emperor.

Christians have grappled for two millennia over why Jesus had to die, and why God didn't come up with a less violent plan for saving humanity from sin.

Among the many explanations, the crucifixion:

- Shows how deadly serious sin is. Since the beginning of humanity, sin has isolated people from God and resulted in death—the death of punished sinners and the death of sacrificed animals.
- Placed Jesus in the company of sinners he came to save—shamed, isolated, and godforsaken.
- Carried out the lethal punishment required for sin, by offering Jesus as an innocent substitute for sinful humanity: "While we were still sinners, Christ died for us" (Romans 5:8).
- Set the stage for the Resurrection—proof that death isn't the end. Witnessing this miracle transformed Jesus' followers from a huddle of cowards in hiding to a bustle of preachers at work on the very streets where Jesus carried his cross a few weeks earlier.

▲ **THEOLOGY OF BLOOD** For Martin Luther, the theologian who reformed the corrupt Christian church, Jesus' crucifixion was a must. "The cross alone is our theology," he wrote, referring to his belief that Jesus died for our sins. "You, Lord Jesus, are my righteousness and I am your sin," Luther once prayed. "You have taken on what you were not, and you have given me what I am not."

► **HOLY SYMBOL OF LOVE**
Pilgrims visiting Jerusalem carry a cross through the streets to mark Good Friday. When Roman emperor Constantine legalized Christianity in the AD 300s and outlawed crucifixion, the cross became a public symbol of Christianity.

◄ **WHERE JESUS DIED** Painting from 1800s of the Church of the Holy Sepulchre. Most Bible experts agree that Jesus was executed and buried on a site marked by the Church of the Holy Sepulchre in Jerusalem. At the time, this area was a used-up quarry turned into a garden and a cemetery, and located just outside the city walls—where the Bible says Jesus was executed. Another less-likely contender is a nearby hilltop with a cliff that resembles the face of a skull. The place Jesus died was called Golgotha, "Skull Hill."

THE LAMB OF GOD

As far as Jews were concerned, "Without the shedding of blood there is no forgiveness" (Hebrews 9:22). After all, they had been sacrificing lambs and other animals for more than 2,000 years before Jesus arrived. John the Baptist introduced Jesus as "the Lamb of God, who takes away the sin of the world!" (John 1:29). And in a vision of end times, another John saw "a Lamb, looking as if it had been slain" (Revelation 5:6). But this Lamb—which most scholars say refers to Jesus—was now very much alive and reigning in heaven. Celestial beings sang: "You were slain, and with your blood you purchased men" (Revelation 5:9).

WHATEVER HAPPENED TO THE TWELVE DISCIPLES?

The Bible reports the death of only two of Jesus' disciples: Judas and James.
   Later church leaders, however, wrote that most of the remaining disciples were martyred because of their religious beliefs.

Simon Peter. His dynamic preaching and miracles launched the Jerusalem church. He later took his preaching on the road. Church leaders say he was crucified in Rome in the AD 60s, when Emperor Nero started persecuting Christians.

Andrew. He is said to have preached in Greece until he was crucified on an X-shaped cross—a design now called St. Andrew's Cross.

James, son of Zebedee. The Bible says he was beheaded about AD 44 at the order of Herod Agrippa, grandson of Herod the Great.

John. Early church leaders said he was the "beloved disciple" Jesus asked to look after his mother. Church tradition also says he wrote the gospel and the three letters bearing his name, along with Revelation. He apparently moved to Ephesus in what is now Turkey, and lived into the AD 90s before dying at a very old age.

Philip. Martyred in Turkey, according to tradition.

Bartholomew. Skinned alive and beheaded in India, according to early Christian writers.

Thomas. Tradition says he was martyred in India.

Matthew. Traditionally considered author of the gospel of Matthew, this former tax collector died a natural death, according to some. Others say he was martyred.

James, son of Alphaeus. It's unknown what happened to him.

Thaddaeus, also known as Judas. Tradition says he was martyred in what is now Iran.

Simon the Zealot. Martyred in Iran with Thaddaeus.

Judas Iscariot. He hung himself, hours after betraying Jesus.

▼ ROMAN DUNGEON

Mamertine Prison was conveniently located a short walk from Rome's Colosseum, where many Christians died as grisly entertainment. Early church writings say Peter and Paul were held in this underground dungeon. Prisoners were dropped through the hole in the ceiling.

ROME BURNS

Two-thirds of Rome burned down in a fire that Emperor Nero—who had said he wanted to renovate the city—was accused of setting in July 64. To divert attention from himself, he reportedly blamed a new and controversial sect: Christians. Among the believers rounded up and executed, according to church tradition, were Peter and Paul. Tradition says Peter was crucified near what is now the Vatican's most famous building—the Church of St. Peter. Paul, a Roman citizen protected from crucifixion, was beheaded.

▲ **LAST SUPPER** During the Last Supper, Jesus, referring to his execution, asked "Can you drink the cup I am going to drink?" "We can," they replied (Matthew 20:22). And most did, according to early church writings.

▼ **PETER CRUCIFIED** The apostle is crucified upside down in Nero's Rome. *Acts of Peter*, a book written by AD 200 at the latest, says Peter was fleeing Rome to escape Christian persecution when he met Jesus walking toward Rome. Peter asked, "Where are you going, Lord?" Jesus replied, "I am going to Rome to be crucified." Peter turned around and was crucified head down at his request, to represent humanity's fallen nature. From the cross he urged the crowd of witnesses to turn from their sins.

◄ **DOUBTING THOMAS IN INDIA** Christians gather for prayer in a Syro-Malabar Catholic Church in India. With more than three million members, the church traces its founding to Thomas. According to their tradition, Thomas arrived on India's southwest coast in what is now the state of Kerala in AD 52. There he started several churches before moving to the east coast where he was martyred.

◀ **DEATH TAKES A RIDE** Death thunders to earth on a pale horse, riding as one of the four horsemen of the Apocalypse in John's end-time vision.

▲ VISION ISLAND The 900-year-old Monastery of Saint John on Patmos island's highest hilltop commemorates John writing Revelation. He wrote this cryptic book from exile on this ten-mile-long Greek island some forty miles off Turkey's coast. Though John didn't identify himself as Jesus' disciple, early church leaders did, adding that John had earlier moved to Ephesus, a leading center of Christianity.

WHY THE BIZARRE SYMBOLS IN END-TIME WRITINGS?

Worshiping God around his throne are creatures "covered with eyes, in the front and the back" (Revelation 4:6).

This strange scene comes from an end-time vision by a prophet named John—the disciple of Jesus, according to church leaders writing in the AD 100s. Several centuries earlier, the prophet Daniel reported similar visions. In both cases, prophets told of extraordinary creatures, and used mystifying symbols and numbers

Though the writing is foreign to us, it was a common literary genre among the Jews and several other Middle Eastern cultures from about 300 BC to AD 200. It was called apocalyptic writing, from the Greek word *apocalypsis*, which means "revelation." Like much of our science fiction writing today, it had code words that most readers of the genre understood. Unfortunately, much of the code has been lost. Some of it, however, can be deciphered once we understand links to the Old Testament and Roman history at the time of the writing.

Apocalyptic writing grew out of hard times. Jews were either in exile or were being oppressed by invaders. Coded language preserved the message of deliverance, the messenger, and the subjugated nation—Rome ruthlessly punished dissident writers and their people.

For today's reader, the writing style has evolved into a mystery. And people love a good mystery. They read it and try to solve it. Though readers today have limited success in breaking the code, the main point comes through with shining clarity: God and his people win, evil loses.

◀ **DOWNTOWN ROME** Ancient Rome's cityscape is dominated by the circular Colosseum amphitheater. *Babylon* was a common code name for Rome. Like Babylon, Rome plundered Israel and leveled the temple.

▲ **CONQUEROR AT WORK** Alexander the Great crushed Persian forces at the Battle of Issus in Turkey—allowing him to quickly dismantle the Persian Empire. Most Bible experts say Alexander was the fast-moving, one-horned goat in Daniel's vision of a future battle between a goat and a ram. "The goat became very great, but at the height of his power his large horn was broken off, and in its place four prominent horns grew up" (Daniel 8:8). Alexander died of a fever in 323 BC at age 33—shortly after arriving in Babylon to build his new capital. Four of his generals carved up the empire.

◀ **DON'T TAKE IT LITERALLY** The angel Gabriel interprets Daniel's bewildering vision of four frightening beasts—one of which was a lion with "the wings of an eagle" (Daniel 7:4). Gabriel said not to take them literally—that the beasts represent four future kingdoms.

BEASTLY ROME

"I saw a beast coming out of the sea.... The dragon gave the beast his power" (Revelation 13:1–2). In his vision, John identifies the dragon as Satan. As for the beast, most scholars say John was referring to the Roman Empire that persecuted Christians. One clue is that this beast crushes the saints and is worshiped throughout the civilized world—perhaps a reference to Caesar, considered a god (13:7–8).

WHY DID PAUL TELL WOMEN TO KEEP QUIET IN CHURCH?

Credited with writing nearly half the books in the New Testament—thirteen of the twenty-seven—Paul takes heavy criticism for two short passages:

- "Women should remain silent in the churches.... If they want to inquire about something, they should ask their own husbands at home" (1 Corinthians 14:34–35).
- "I do not permit a woman to teach or to have authority over a man; she must be silent" (1 Timothy 2:12).

This perplexes Bible experts because it appears to be the exact opposite of what Paul said elsewhere. He commended many female ministers: Phoebe, Lydia, Euodia, Syntyche, Priscilla, and Junias. Priscilla tutored famed preacher Apollos. And some Bible experts say Junias seemed to have risen not only to the church's top rank of apostle—but was "outstanding among the apostles" (Romans 16:7). Other experts argue that Paul didn't mean Junias was an apostle. Instead, he was using the informal meaning of the word, "one who was sent."

Paul's apparent inconsistency has spawned many ideas about why he told women to keep quiet in church.

Chauvinist editor. Some scholars say someone added this to Paul's writing, though every ancient manuscript includes the statements.

Protecting marriage. Some scholars say Paul was trying to preserve marriages by advising wives not to publicly debate religion with their husbands.

Two troubled churches. Some say Paul was addressing just two congregations where women were stirring up trouble. His rules didn't apply elsewhere.

Many denominations today allow women preachers, but it's the rare church that hires one. Some churches, especially among Southern Baptists—America's largest denomination—refuse to hire them. These churches represent what scholars call the complementarian view, which says that though men and women are equal, they have different functions to fulfill in the home and the church.

◄ **EVE BEFORE ADAM** Women in Ephesus may have embraced a Gnostic heresy that said God created Eve first. Some scholars say Paul's use of the rare word referring to women taking "authority" over a man could also mean "proclaiming oneself originator." If so, that might help explain Paul's next sentence: "For Adam was formed first, then Eve" (1 Timothy 2:13).

▶ **GUARDIANS NEEDED** Funeral portraits of women from Paul's time, about AD 50. Women in Roman times—whether Jewish or Roman—were treated as minors. They couldn't even make out a will because they usually weren't allowed to own property. For all of their lives most women remained under the control of men, first their fathers, then husbands, and then as a widow under the care of sons or other male relatives.

◄ **PROGRESSIVE PAUL** Many scholars say Paul helped turn the corner on women's rights by declaring, "There is neither Jew nor Greek, slave nor free, male nor female, for you are all one in Christ Jesus" (Galatians 3:28).

◄ **LETTING HER LIGHT SHINE** An American Quaker named Sarah Grimke (1792–1873) spoke out against slavery in public lectures. When Christian leaders said she shouldn't address men in public, she argued that Jesus told crowds of men *and* women that it was wrong for people to hide their light under a basket. "Whatever is right for man to do," she wrote, "is right for woman."

TROUBLE SPOTS

Paul ordered women to keep quiet in a pair of churches located in two of Rome's largest cities, Corinth and Ephesus. In Corinth, women may have been speaking in unknown tongues without an interpreter or causing other noisy confusion.

Aegean Sea

GREECE
• Corinth

TURKEY
• Ephesus

The Mediterranean Sea

IS A PLANET-KILLING APOCALYPSE COMING?

"I will sweep away everything from the face of the earth," declares the Lord. "I will sweep away both men and animals" (Zephaniah 1:2–3).

This obscure prophet wasn't the only one in the Bible predicting the end of life on earth. Isaiah—in a section of the Bible experts call the Apocalypse of Isaiah—said God would "lay waste the earth and devastate it" (Isaiah 24:1). Yet another prophet in a vision of the future said he saw a new earth—"the first earth had passed away" (Revelation 21:1).

These predictions, however, appear in a genre of writing—apocalyptic—famed for its poetry and symbolism. If we take the predictions literally, some scholars warn, we could wind up dead wrong—as wrong as the ancient Jews, so prophecy-programmed by their notion of what the messiah would be like that they didn't recognize him when he came.

Some end-time descriptions in the Bible might refer to what is now part of Israel's sad history, such as Babylon leveling Jerusalem and wiping the Jewish nation off the map. Perhaps some prophecies refer to spiritual consequences instead of physical ones. And maybe some do refer to a physical disaster as cataclysmic as the flood.

This much appears certain. In each doomsday prophecy, the story of God's people doesn't end in tragedy. They survive in God's new creation.

The Bible doesn't answer most of our questions about that new creation—the when, where, or how. But Jesus did answer the "who" question by assuring his followers that they could trust him. As Jesus got ready to return to his heavenly kingdom, he told his disciples, "I am going there to prepare a place for you. And if I go and prepare a place for you, I will come back and take you to be with me that you also may be where I am" (John 14:2–3).

▶ **NERO 666** Some Bible experts speculate that the beast of Revelation was Nero, the Roman emperor who started persecuting Christians. "If anyone has insight, let him calculate the number of the beast, for it is man's number. His number is 666" (Revelation 13:18). In Greek, the international language of the day, letters had number equivalents (A=1, B=2). Letters of Nero's name and title—Caesar Nero—total 666.

MISTAKEN APOCALYPSE

Albert Schweitzer, a famous theologian, medical missionary, and musician who died in 1965, argued that Jesus wrongly expected the world to end soon when he said, "This generation will certainly not pass away until all these things have happened" (Matthew 24:34). Some scholars defended Jesus by swinging to the other extreme, insisting that Jesus fulfilled his end-time predictions. Many scholars today, however, argue that Jesus was talking about the beginning of a new era—called end-times—which started at the crucifixion and will end with the second coming. These experts argue that the end has started, and there's more to come.

▲ **SONS OF LIGHT** Found inside this cave near the Dead Sea was one of the famous Dead Sea Scrolls, the Community Rule, which reads like a constitution. It was preserved by a group of monk-like Jews who lived during the first Christian century and waited anxiously for the Apocalypse. This and other scrolls show that they thought of themselves as "Sons of Light" who would join God's army to fight the "Sons of Darkness," which they considered the Romans. Ironically, Romans destroyed the settlement in AD 68 while crushing a nationwide Jewish uprising.

▼ **PERFECT BATTLEFIELD** When Napoleon arrived at the sprawling Valley of Armageddon, he declared it the world's most perfect battlefield. Called Jezreel Valley by the locals, it stretches for twenty miles along the foot of the Carmel Mountains in northern Israel. Here is where some believe heaven's armies will wipe out the armies of earth. But it's unclear if John of Revelation was pointing to this valley. *Armageddon* appears only once in the Bible, but the closest Hebrew meaning seems to be *Har Megiddo*, meaning "mountain of Megiddo." Megiddo, as seen below, was a hilltop fortress overlooking the valley.

WHEN WILL JESUS RETURN?

As the disciples stared up into the sky, watching Jesus ascend to his heavenly kingdom, they probably never would have guessed that Christians today would still be waiting for him to come back.

They had good reason to expect the second coming in their lifetime.

Jesus himself detailed end-time events, including "the Son of Man coming on the clouds of the sky, with power and great glory," adding that "this generation will certainly not pass away until all these things have happened" (Matthew 24:30, 33). Many scholars today, however, say the events of "this generation" referred only to the Roman destruction of Jerusalem about forty years after Jesus, in AD 70.

Yet even Paul, early in his ministry, talked about Jesus coming back soon. In one of his first letters, he wrote that when Jesus returns, the dead will rise first. "After that, we who are still alive and are left will be caught up together with them in the clouds to meet the Lord in the air" (1 Thessalonians 4:17).

As decades passed, the Apostle Peter explained Jesus' delay. "With the Lord a day is like a thousand years, and a thousand years are like a day. The Lord is not slow in keeping his promise. . . . He is patient with you, not wanting anyone to perish, but everyone to come to repentance" (2 Peter 3:8–9).

First generation Christians grew old and started dying. Leaders urged the next generation to hold onto their hope of the second coming, but to focus less on the waiting and more on the work—reminding them of Jesus' parting words, "Be my witnesses in Jerusalem, and in all Judea and Samaria, and to the ends of the earth" (Acts 1:8).

DATE-SETTERS

Though Jesus said he would come unexpectedly—like a thief at night—many Christians have sifted Bible prophecies for nuggets of news. Here are a few predicted dates of Jesus' return.

1836. German Lutheran theologian John Bengel (1687–1752) predicted this is when Jesus' thousand-year reign would begin.

1843. Farmer-turned-lecturer William Miller reached this date of the second coming by speculating that the 2,300 days in Daniel 8:14 meant years from 457 BC—the date Miller said the Persian king freed Jews from exile.

1844. Miller bumped the date back a year after Jesus didn't show, saying he forgot about the year 0. Though he was wrong again, the excitement he generated produced the Seventh-Day Adventist Church.

1988. Hal Lindsey, author of *The Late Great Planet Earth,* said Jesus would return by this date—forty years after the rebirth of Israel. He based that on Jesus saying the end would come within a "generation" of the signs described in Matthew 24. D. Edgar Whisenant, author of 88 Reasons Why the Rapture Will Be in 1988, also picked this date.

1989. Whisenant said he miscalculated by a year.

October 28, 1992. South Korean minister Jang Rim Lee predicted this date for the return of Jesus. End-time hysteria swept over the country. Afterward, police arrested Lee for fraud, charging he had collected more than four million dollars—some of which he invested in bonds maturing in 1993.

◄ SIGNS OF THE TIME With the first test explosion of an atomic bomb in 1945, people suddenly realized humanity was capable of fulfilling one end-time prophecy: "the earth and everything in it will be laid bare" (2 Peter 3:10). Three years later, after a 2,000-year absence, Israel was suddenly restored—an apparent answer to God's rhetorical question, "Can a country be born in a day?" (Isaiah 66:8). And after the first television satellite was launched in 1962, many people said they understood how when Jesus returns, "every eye will see him" (Revelation 1:7).

► TO STOP A MESSIAH
Jerusalem's sealed east gate. Arab invaders sealed up the gateway to stop the messiah. Many Christians say Jesus will return to the Mount of Olives, since that's where he ascended and where angels told the disciples Jesus would "come back in the same way you have seen him go" (Acts 1:11). Jews say the messiah will enter Jerusalem from the Mount of Olives side of the city "through the gate facing east" (Ezekiel 43:4).

IS HELL REAL OR A SYMBOL?

Hell is a fiery place of never-ending torture—no more symbolic than falling into a volcano. That's the traditional view.

Fuel for that theological fire comes from many Bible passages, none more searing than the words of Jesus, "As the weeds are pulled up and burned in the fire, so it will be at the end of the age" (Matthew 13:40).

To many Christians, that seems harsh because the torture serves no helpful purpose. So they've come up with less traditional ideas about hell.

There's no fire, just the torment of separation from God. Descriptions of hell are symbolic of eternal separation from God, evidenced by images of "darkness" (Matthew 8:12) and "fire"—though fire burns away darkness.

Fire symbolizes annihilation. The Bible's most common word for hell was Gehenna, a valley just outside Jerusalem thought to have been the city dump. God throws sinners in the trash, destroying them. It's the destruction, not the suffering, that's eternal. Paul said, "The wages of sin is death" (Romans 6:23).

Everyone will be saved eventually. God will keep sinners alive in the next life, until they come to their spiritual senses. His goal in the next life—as in this—is reconciliation. If rebel souls still exist, even in hell, then God hasn't been able "to reconcile to himself all things" (Colossians 1:19).

These varied theories show how hard it is for physical beings to understand spiritual realities. There's no frame of reference. But no matter which theory people prefer, the message of the Bible is that everyone who seeks the Lord will find him. And it won't be in hell.

► SIN DEMANDS HELL
American preacher Jonathan Edwards (1703–1758) wrote, "It is a most unreasonable thing to suppose that there should be no future punishment, to suppose that God ... should let man alone ... and never punish him for his sins, and never make any difference between the good and the bad."

HELL ON EARTH
Jerusalem in the 1800s. The small valley just south of the hilltop were Jews once worshiped at the Jerusalem temple is the place where hell gets its name. When Jesus spoke of hell, he used the word *Gehenna*, from the Hebrew words *ge hinnom*, meaning "valley of Hinnom." This is where Jewish kings Ahaz and Manasseh burned their children in sacrifice to idols—sins that contributed to the nation's collapse. Just as Sodom became synonymous with sin, Gehenna became synonymous with fiery punishment for sin.

Jerusalem

Mt. of Olives

Hinnom Valley (Gehenna)

Kidron Valley

▲ NEVER-ENDING FIRE
Hell-bound souls of the evil dead are painted as ending up in a place that suits their spirit. Jesus talked about hell more than anyone else in the Bible. He described it as a place of eternal torment, "where the fire never goes out" (Mark 9:43).

◄ CHRIST'S MORAL DEFECT British philosopher Bertrand Russell (1872–1970) wrote, "There is one very serious defect to my mind in Christ's moral character, and that is that he believed in hell. I do not myself feel that any person who is really profoundly humane can believe in everlasting punishment."

PHOTO CREDITS

All maps are © Mosaic Graphics

1–Where Was the Garden of Eden?

Painting of Eve	Giraudon/Art Resource, NY
Fruit stand	Tor Eigeland/Saudi Aramco World
Iranian mountains	© Topham/The Image Works
Tabriz	© Topham/The Image Works
Armed angel	Image Select/Art Resource, NY
First mention of Eden	University of Pennsylvania Museum

2–Did People Really Live Hundreds of Years?

Sumerian king list	Ashmolean Museum, Oxford
Moses	Erich Lessing/Art Resource, NY
Angel	Scala/Art Resource, NY
Tiny worm	Zeynep F. Altun/Wikimedia

3–Was There a World-Wide Flood?

Gilgamesh epic	Todd Bolen/www.BiblePlaces.com
Zeus	Scala/Art Resource, NY
Bosporus Strait	Courtesy of NASA

4–Whatever Happened to Noah's Ark?

Ararat from space	Courtesy of NASA
Ararat	Courtesy of NASA
Mount Ararat wood	Elfred Lee
Noah's ark dimensions	© The Zondervan Corporation
Noah's barge	R Walsh @ ww.noahs-ark.net

5–What Was the Tower of Babel?

Clay cylinder	© Marie-Lan Nguyen/Wikimedia Commons
Tower of Babel	Erich Lessing/Art Resource, NY
Babylon's Tower of Babel	Courtesy of the Oriental Institute of the University of Chicago
Tower in Abraham's hometown	Mcdermott, John R. (Connecticut)/National Geographic Image Collection
Reconstructed wall	Michael Spencer/Saudi Aramco World/PADIA

6–Why Circumcision As a Symbol of God's Promise to Abraham?

Angry circumcision	Michelangelo/Planet Art
Joyful family occasion	Z. Radovan/www.BibleLandPictures.com
Tools of circumcision	Z. Radovan/www.BibleLandPictures.com
Jewish and ashamed	Alinari/Art Resource, NY
Philo	Special Collections Library, University of Michigan
Sign of God's covenant	Titan/Planet Art

7–What Happened to Sodom and Gomorrah?

Sodom on fire	Kavaler/Art Resource, NY
Earthquake zone	© The Zondervan Corporation
Salt pillars	Z. Radovan/www.BibleLandPictures.com
Dead Sea with salt	Steven Allen/www.istockphoto.com
Oil jelly icebergs	Illustration by Bob Lapsley/Saudi Aramco World/PADIA

8–Were the Plagues of Egypt Natural Disasters?

Egypt's unnamed pharaoh	© The British Museum/HIP/The Image Works
No rays from Re	© Topham/The Image Works
Akhenation	Erich Lessing/Art Resource, NY
Egypt's plague report	Erich Lessing/Art Resource, NY
Swarm of locusts	© Aladin Abdel Naby/Reuters/Corbis

9–How Large was the Exodus Crowd?

"Israel is wiped out"	Z. Radovan/www.BibleLandPictures.com
Kadesh Barnea	Z. Radovan/www.BibleLandPictures.com
Builder king	HIP/Art Resource, NY
A swarm of Hebrews	© Corporation of London/HIP/The Image Works

10–Did the Red Sea Really Part?

Moses was here?	Erich Lessing/Art Resource, NY
Napoleon's Red Sea crossing	Erich Lessing/Art Resource, NY
Ramses II	Todd Bolen/www.BiblePlaces.com
Parting the water	Scala/Art Resource, NY

11–Why Did the Israelites Worship a Golden Calf?

Mountain of Moses	Z. Radovan/www.BibleLandPictures.com
Bull riding	Z. Radovan/www.BibleLandPictures.com
Golden calf	Copyright 1995-2008 Phoenix Data Systems
Babylon's 282 commandments	Erich Lessing/Art Resource, NY
Calf worship	Scala/Art Resource, NY
Moses with horns	Erich Lessing/Art Resource, NY

12–Why did God require Blood Sacrifices?

Sacrifices for all occasions	Scala/Art Resource, NY
Jewish altar	Copyright 1995-2008 Phoenix Data Systems
Continuing the tradition	Z. Radovan/www.BibleLandPictures.com
Sacrifice to end all sacrifices	Caravaggio/Planet Art
Sir Edward Tylor	Oxford University Museum of Natural History
Adam and Eve	Alinari/Regione Umbria/Art Resource, NY

13–Why Kosher Food?

Pigs for demons	Réunion des Musées Nationaux/Art Resource, NY
Fish bargaining	Bill Aron
Man carrying meat on shoulder	© Topham/The Image Works
Caesar Augustus	Cameraphoto Arte, Venice/Art Resource, NY
End of kosher	Erich Lessing/Art Resource, NY

14–Where did the Manna and Quail come from?

Badlands of Sin	NASA/World Wind
Carving of gathering manna	Alinari/SEAT/Art Resource, NY
Painting of Israelites gathering manna	Réunion des Musées Nationaux/Art Resource, NY
Manna from sap	Photo by Jack Deloach
Quail	© Topham/The Image Works
Hieroglyphics	Erich Lessing/Art Resource, NY

15–Why Didn't God Let Moses into the Promised Land?

Water in the rock	Scala/Art Resource, NY
Glimpsing the promised land	Erich Lessing/Art Resource, NY
Moses sees the promised land	The Jewish Museum, NY/Art Resource, NY
Seti I	Erich Lessing/Art Resource, NY
Burning bushes	Richard Nowitz

16–Why Did God Order All Canaanites Slaughtered?

Canaanite from Joshua's day	Erich Lessing/Art Resource, NY
Astarte	Giraudon/Art Resource, NY
Canaanite silver idos	Erich Lessing/Art Resource, NY
Altar at Megiddo	Stephen M. Miller
Hebrews take high ground	The Jewish Museum, NY/Art Resource, NY

17–Did the Walls of Jericho Really Come Tumblin' Down?

City walls	Illustration by Mark Sheeres
Bump in the valley	Z. Radovan/www.BibleLandPictures.com
Jericho walls cross-section	© The Zondervan Corporation
Jars full of grain	Z. Radovan/www.BibleLandPictures.com

18–Did the Sun and Moon Stop During Joshua's Battle?

Sun stand still	The Jewish Museum, NY/Art Resource, NY
Hail	Samuel Zinn
Shafted	Erich Lessing/Art Resource, NY
Shadows in reverse	Scala/Art Resource, NY

19–What Happened to the Ark of the Covenant?

A model of the ark	Z. Radovan/www.BibleLandPictures.com
Ark's footprint	Public domain
Synagogue arks	Z. Radovan/www.BibleLandPictures.com
God's throne on earth	Courtesy of the Library of Congress

20–Why Did a Chariot of Fire Take Elijah to Heaven?

Elijah in chariot of fire	Giuseppe Angeli, Elijah Taken Up in a Chariot of Fire, Samuel H. Kress Collection, Image © 2007 Board of Trustees, National Gallery of Art, Washington
Warrior prophet	Stephen M. Miller
Elijah's chair	Z. Radovan/www.BibleLandPictures.com
Elijah's cup	Richard Nowitz
Church of the Transfiguration	© www.gregschneider.com

21–How Could Isaiah Accurately Describe Jesus-700 years BC?

Isaiah's suffering servant	Erich Lessing/Art Resource, NY
Nation of suffering servants	Stephen M. Miller
Isaiah's scroll	Z. Radovan/www.BibleLandPictures.com
Rabbi Menachem Mendel Schneerson	AP Photo/Mike Albans
Selah coins	Z. Radovan/www.BibleLandPictures.com

22–Did a Big Fish Really Swallow Jonah?

Jonah's sea cruise	Bayer & Mitko-Artothek
Sperm whale	© Topham/The Image Works
Philistine ship	Z. Radovan/www.BibleLandPictures.com
Modern Jonah	Public domain

23–Does Prayer Change God's Mind?

Jesus in garden of Gethsemane	Scala/Art Resource, NY
Soren Kierkegaard	The Royal Library, Copenhagen, Department of Maps, Prints and Photographs
Prayer tour	© www.gregschneider.com
Against the wall	Bill Aron
Angel	© Topham/The Image Works

24–What Happened to Israel's Lost Tribes?

Wandering Jews	Erich Lessing/Art Resource, NY
African Jews	© Zbigniew Bzdak/The Image Works
Josephus	© ARPL/Topham/The Image Works
Indian girl	Z. Radovan/www.BibleLandPictures.com

25–What was the Star of Bethlehem?

Strangers bearing gifts	Cameraphoto/Art Resource, NY
Pope Gregory XIII	Scala/Art Resource, NY
Gold	Erich Lessing/Art Resource, NY
Frankincense	Dick Doughty/Saudi Aramco World/PADIA
Myrrh	Z. Radovan/www.BibleLandPictures.com
Angel visiting sheperds	Stephen M. Miller
Bethlehem star	Stephen M. Miller

26–Was Mary Really a Virgin When She Delivered Jesus?

Mary and Jesus	Erich Lessing/Art Resource, NY
Christ's house	Tate Gallery, London/Art Resource, NY
Hercules	Scala/Art Resource, NY
Aramaic inscription	Erich Lessing/Art Resource, NY
Teen mother	Katrina Thomas/Saudi Aramco World/PADIA

27–Why Are Shady Women Listed in Jesus' Family Tree?

Widow	Stephen M. Miller
Bedouin woman	© Norbert Schiller/The Image Works
Humanitarian prostitute	The Jewish Museum/Art Resource, NY
Bathsheba	Cameraphoto/Art Resource, NY
Four terrible sinners	Caravaggio/Planet Art

28–Why Didn't Jesus Want to Turn Water into Wine at Cana?

The last shall be best	Erich Lessing/Art Resource, NY
Jug of cold water	© The British Museum/HIP/The Image Works
Wedding blessing over wine	Bill Aron
Dionysus holding a cup	© AAAC/Topham/The Image Works
Wedding buffet	Kristie Burns/Saudi Aramco World/PADIA

29–Is the Devil a Living Being, or a Symbol of Evil?

Auschwitz concentration camp	© Topham/The Image Works
Bottled demon	© Fortean/Topham/The Image Works
Pact with a demon	© Charles Walker/Topham/The Image Works
Exorcism	© Charles Walker/Topham/The Image Works
John Wesley	© Topham/The Image Works
Fallen angel	Smithsonian American Art Museum, Washington, DC/Art Resource, NY

30–Why Does God Let Bad Things Happen?

Mount Vesuvius victim	Werner Forman/Art Resource, NY
Pierre Bayle	Réunion des Musées Nationaux/Art Resource, NY
St. Augustine	© Topham/The Image Works
Job's total loss	Réunion des Musées Nationaux/Art Resource, NY
Slave becomes a savior	The Jewish Museum/Art Resource, NY

31–How Can There Be Three Gods in One?

Three for the baptism	Cameraphoto Arte, Venice/Art Resource, NY
Woman being baptized	Stephen M. Miller
St. Ambrose	Réunion des Musées Nationaux/Art Resource, NY
Miracles instead of an explanation	Scala/Art Resource, NY
Majority opinion	Scala/Art Resource, NY
Egyptian heretic, Arius	© AAAC/Topham/The Image Works

32–What Is the Unforgivable Sin?

Bust of Plato	Scala/Art Resource, NY
Drop-dead disobedience	Victoria & Albert Museum, London/Art Resource, NY
Holy Spirit decends	© Topham/The Image Works
Scholars as critics	Bill Aron
Sermon on the Mount	Réunion des Musées Nationaux/Art Resource, NY

33–Why did Judas Betray Jesus?

Kiss of death	A.M. Rosati/Art Resource, NY
Garden of Gethsemane	© www.gregschneider.com
Blood money coins	Z. Radovan/www.BibleLandPictures.com
Satan at the last supper	Tate Gallery, London/Art Resource, NY
The Temple scroll	Z. Radovan/www.BibleLandPictures.com

34–Why did Jesus have to Die?

Christ on the Cross	Erich Lessing/Art Resource, NY
Shepherd with sheep	© www.gregschneider.com
Martin Luther preaching	© Topham/The Image Works
Holy symbol of love	Z. Radovan/www.BibleLandPictures.com
Church of the Holy Sepulchre	Painting by David Roberts. Courtesy of the Library of Congress.

35–Whatever Happened to the Twelve Disciples?

Praying in India	© Sean Sprague/The Image Works
Peter crucified upsidedown	Caravaggio/Planet Art
Rome burns	Giraudon/Art Resource, NY
Roman dungeon	© www.gregschneider.com
A few good fishermen	Armitage, Edward/The Bridgeman Art Library
Last Supper	Titian/Art Resource, NY

36–Why the Bizarre Symbols in End-Time Writings?

Beastly Rome	Alinari/Art Resource, NY

Downtown Rome	Scala/Art Resource, NY
Alexander the Great	© CM Dixon/HIP/The Image Works
Death takes a ride	Cameraphoto Arte, Venice/ Art Resource, NY
Monastery of St. John	Copyright 1995-2008 Phoenix Data Systems
Winged beast statue	© The British Museum/HIP/ The Image Works

37–Why did Paul tell Women to Keep Quiet in Church?

Egyptian woman	Erich Lessing/Art Resource, NY
Egyptian woman	Erich Lessing/Art Resource, NY
Progressive Paul	National Trust/Art Resource, NY
Paul preaching	Cameraphoto/Art Resource, NY
Sarah Grimke	Courtesy of the Library of Congress
Adam and Eve	The Jewish Museum, NY/ Art Resource, NY

38–Is a Planet-Killing Apocalypse Coming?

Albert Schweitzer	Courtesy of the Library of Congress
Qumran cave	Copyright 1995-2008 Phoenix Data Systems
Nero	Erich Lessing/Art Resource, NY
Meteor	© Topham/The Image Works
Perfect battlefield	Copyright 1995-2008 Phoenix Data Systems

39–When Will Jesus Return?

Jewish graveyard	© www.gregschneider.com
Jerusalem's East Gate	Courtesy of the Library of Congress
Second coming	Scala/Art Resource, NY
Nagaski atomic bomb	© Topham/The Image Works
William Miller	William Miller, courtesy of the Jenks Memorial Collection of Adventual Materials, Aurora University

40–Is Hell Real or a Symbol?

Bertrand Russell	© Topham/The Image Works
Hell on earth	Courtesy of the Library of Congress
Jonathan Edwards	Courtesy of the Library of Congress
Never-ending fire	Scala/Art Resource, NY
Woman and demon	Scala/Art Resource, NY
People boiling in pots	© Topham/The Image Works

We want to hear from you. Please send your comments about this book to us in care of zreview@zondervan.com. Thank you.

ZONDERVAN.com/
AUTHORTRACKER
follow your favorite authors